# PUBLICATIONS

## PAQUETTE

# 1st Edition
## Abridged Version

# Simple Limited Power of Attorney

Power of Attorney (POA only) for
Your Estate Planning Needs

## Paul M. Paquette

# FIRST EDITION (Abridged Version)

© 2018, 2019

| | | | | | | |
|---|---|---|---|---|---|---|
| Book Design: | Paul M. Paquette | Proofread: | Paul M. Paquette | CD/USB: | Paul M. Paquette |
| Front Cover: | Paul M. Paquette | Editor: | Paul M. Paquette | Printing: | N/A |
| Back Cover: | Paul M. Paquette | Glossary: | Paul M. Paquette | Company: | Paquette Publications |
| Cover Photo: | Marcela | Index: | N/A | Location: | Auburn, KY - USA |

**Author:** Paquette, Paul M.

**Title:** Simple Limited Power of Attorney

**Subtitle:** Power of Attorney (POA Only) For Your Estate Planning Needs

**Identifiers:** 978-1-948389-69-3 PB | 978-1-948389-91-4 HC | 978-1-948389-80-8 EBK: PDF |

**Classification:** Unabridged LCCN: 2018900398 | DDC: 346.7302/9—dc23 |

**Subject:** 1. Law | 2. Power of Attorney | 3. Practical Guides | 4. Estate Planning

**PCIP:**
Paquette, Paul., 1982 –
Simple Limited Power of Attorney:
Power of Attorney (POA Only) For Your Estate Planning Needs (Estate Planning Series)
by Paul Paquette --1st ed.--Auburn, KY.: Paquette Publications. c2018, c2019
ISBN - 13: 978-1-948389-69-3 (PB).          -- ISBN - 13: 978-1-948389-91-4 (HC).
ISBN - 13: 978-1-948389-80-8 (EBK: PDF).
1. Power of attorney--United States--Popular works. 2. Power of attorney--United States--Forms.
3. Estate Planning--United States--Popular works.  4. Estate planning--United States--Forms. I. Title II. Series

**Special Note:** Previously Titled as **"Simple Power of Attorney."**

Summary: The book consists of (**01**) one Simple Power of Attorney (**Limited**). This Power of Attorney focuses on estate planning and provides options, depth, and flexibility while maintaining uniformity with built-in and optional (Durability Provisions) safety features.

**Publication Media:** Paquette Publications publishes in various formats (print, electronic, and print-on-demand). Some independent purchases or material included with the standard print versions may not be available in e-books or print-on-demand. If physical media (CD, DVD, or USB Drive) is not available within the book, then said files are downloadable online in digital format.

**Digital Formats:** Power of Attorney, Supporting Documents, Forms (Miscellaneous / Recommended), Worksheets, and Appendices are available in the following digital formats (PDF, DOCX, DOC, and ODT).

**Bulk Purchases:** Purchases of titles by Paquette Publications may occur in bulk for educational, business, fund-raising, or sale promotional use. For information, please email the following: **paquettepublications@gmail.com**.

**Questions:** Please send all questions, suggestions, comments, and permission requests to the following email: **paquettepublications@gmail.com**.

**Please Note:** The purpose of this Publication(s) and its design is to provide accurate and authoritative information concerning the subject matter covered. The author has striven to use simple/plain English to clarify complex issues and make understanding/comprehension usable and intuitive. Due to the changing nature of law in the United States of America, the author makes the following **Legal Disclaimers & Waivers** on page iv.

# Legal Disclaimers & Waivers

**Definitions of Terms:** The term "Publication(s)" shall refer, but are not limited, to the following: Power of Attorney, Supporting Documents, Worksheets, Miscellaneous Forms, Recommended Forms, and Appendices.

**Waiver of Damages:** The Purchaser or User of this Publication(s) agrees by default and understands the following: (**01**) The Organization, Distributor, Sales Representative, Publisher, or Author makes no guarantees of any kind or nature. (**02**) The Organization, Distributor, Sales Representative, Publisher, or Author assumes no liability for any or all damages resulting from utilizing this Publication(s) or reliance thereof. (**03**) Modification of this Publication(s) is permissible to suit a particular Purchaser or User need; however, the Purchaser or User assumes all risk.

**No Representation of Services:** The Purchaser or User of this Publication(s) agrees by default and understands the following: (**01**) The Organization, Distributor, Sales Representative, Publisher, or Author is not engaged in rendering professional services regarding medical, financial, legal, et cetera. (**02**) This Publication(s) is not a substitute for advice from a competent licensed professional.

**Forum – Selection / Jurisdiction / Governing Law:** The Purchaser or User of this Publication(s) agrees by default and understands the following: (**01**) The selection for governing law, venue, forum, and jurisdiction for all litigation shall exclusively be at the locality of the Organization (State of Incorporation) or the Author (State of Residence). (**02**) The Purchaser or User waives their right to choose, object, or make claims (economic hardship, unreasonable constraints, or inconvenience) concerning the governing law, venue, forum, and jurisdiction for all litigation against the Organization, Distributor, Sales Representative, Publisher, or Author. (**03**) Furthermore, the governing law, venue, forum, and jurisdiction may be further restricted based on City and County; please refer to "Additional Terms & Conditions" for more information.

**Force / Mandatory Arbitration:** The Purchaser or User of this Publication(s) agrees by default and understands the following: (**01**) All litigation, claims, disputes, settlements, judgments, lawsuits, or proceedings (governmental, administrative, governmental investigation, inquiries, hearing, request, or any appeal thereof) against the Organization, Distributor, Sales Representative, Publisher, or Author shall only go through force and binding arbitration with no other alternative legal recourse. (**02**) The arbitration shall be confidential in adherence to the Commercial Arbitration Rules of the American Arbitration Association. (**03**) Any judgment on the award rendered by the Arbitrator may be entered in any court having jurisdiction thereof or having jurisdiction over the relevant party or its assets. (**04**) The arbitration shall be performed by one (**01**) mutually agreed upon Arbitrator with experience in contract law. The arbitration shall be in English. (**05**) The Purchaser or User shall bear their costs in the arbitration with no right or award for reimbursement.

**Injunctive Relief:** The Purchaser or User agrees by default and understands that unauthorized access to or use of this Publication(s) that violates the limited or commercial license shall result in injunctive remedies (or an equivalent type of urgent legal relief) in any jurisdiction without providing notice or opportunity to cure.

**Aggregate Liability:** The Purchaser or User of this Publication(s) agrees by default and understands that the total aggregate liability arising out of or in connection with your use of or inability to use the Paquette Publications websites or Content contained thereon (whether in contract, tort, or otherwise) shall not exceed the monetary amount received by the Organization, Distributor, Sales Representative, Publisher, or Author from the Purchaser or User.

**Class Action Waiver:** The Purchaser or User of this Publication(s) agrees by default and understands the following: (**01**) To bring only claims in an individual capacity, not as a Class Member/Plaintiff/Petitioner in any class, consolidation, or proceeding (mass or representative). (**02**) The Arbitrator shall not consolidate more than one person's claim nor preside over any form of class, consolidation, or proceeding (mass or representative) unless the Defendant/Respondent agrees in writing to such actions in advance.

**Additional Terms & Conditions:** The Purchaser or User of this Publication(s) agrees by default and understands that their legal and consumer rights are restricted and legally bound to any/all updated Additional Terms & Conditions set forth on **www.paquettepublications.com** without prior or future notice. The Additional Terms & Conditions URL links are at the bottom of the home page: Legal Disclaimers & Waivers, License & Trademark, and All Rights Reserved.

**Note of Caution:** When filling out this Publication(s), please consider the following. The Purchaser or User should seek a legal professional's advice if the Purchaser or User is less than eighteen (18) years of age and currently deemed mentally incompetent or incapacitated. Feel free to utilize this Publication(s) as a template. However, without legal representation in the situation above, this Publication(s) would suffer litigation by Interested Third Parties and more than likely receive judgment as invalid. Remember, an active lawful court order covering the subject matter within this Publication(s) will always take precedence if a conflict occurs. **Please Note:** If the Purchaser or User does have an active court order. The Purchaser or User can design this Publication(s), so it is not in conflict; however, seek the advice of a legal professional if there are any questions.

**Legal Questions:** Practicing law without a license is a crime that comes with some hefty fines in the United States of America. To avoid the appearance of impropriety, the Author will not dispense any legal advice or provide any legal services. Furthermore, no Author of any self-help legal book will willfully give legal advice or services due to liability reasons. If the Purchaser or User has a legal question(s), seek out the advice of a competent licensed Attorney.

# PUBLICATIONS

PAQUETTE

"Nothing is impossible to him who will try." ~ Alexander the Great

v

## Paul M. Paquette

Is a Western Kentucky University alumnus with a Financial Planning and Management degree.

He is a military veteran in the United States Army with eight years of experience as a Financial Management Technician.

Insurance & Securities License.

Free Thinker & Entrepreneur.

Favorite hobbies include coin collecting, watching movies, genealogy, camping, hiking, fishing, reading, and cooking.

# PUBLICATIONS

# AQUETTE

"Life is really simple, but we insist on making it complicated." ~ Confucius

# Overview & Perspective

**Importance of Agent(s) Selection:** In the Author's opinion, a Power of Attorney (POA) is the most powerful legal document a person can execute for estate planning purposes. Thus, the Principal should think long and hard when choosing an Agent. The Principal should seek a **Reliable**, **Trustworthy**, and **Competent** Agent(s). Do not shirk in doing one's due diligence regarding Agent selections; if doubts or concerns exist, suggest utilizing the various optional safety features available within the POA.

**Categories of POA:** The Author breaks down a POA into the following four categories: **(01)** Simple, **(02)** Complex, **(03)** Durable, and **(04)** Special. A **Simple POA** is for short-term (less than five years) use with an Agent whose honor is beyond reproach and doubt. A **Complex POA** is for long-term (greater than five years) use, preferably with multiple Agents to reflect the changing realities of life with optional safety features that create additional administrative burdens but with checks and balances on the Agent's power. A **Durable POA** is, in essence, a Complex POA; however, the durability provisions are already active. A **Special POA** is, in essence, a Simple POA best used spartanly with a limited scope and purpose.

**Various Type of POA:** Within the various categories of POA are the following types that the Author has written or plans to write so far:

- **Simple POA:**     **(01)** Limited, **(02)** Banking, **(03)** Financial, **(04)** General, **(05)** Real Estate, and **(06)** Minor.

- **Complex POA:**   **(01)** Limited, **(02)** Banking, **(03)** Financial, **(04)** General, **(05)** Real Estate, and **(06)** Minor.

- **Durable POA:**     **(01)** Protecting, **(02)** Final Disposition, **(03)** Health Care, and **(04)** Health Care of Minor.

- **Special POA:**      **(01)** Taxes, **(02)** Vehicles, and **(03)** Pets.

**Principal:** A Principal is a person who establishes a POA. The Principal names an Agent and bestows that person the ability to perform actions on the Principal's behalf.

**Agent:** An Agent serves in a fiduciary capacity on behalf of the Principal. This fiduciary position is usually voluntary. Monetary compensation and reimbursement usually occur if the Principal has the financial means. The POA outlines the Agent's powers along with any goals and objectives.

**Supporting Documents:** These supporting documents accompany the POA for administrative purposes; these documents are optional (may be required). The Agent's forms are as follows: **(01)** **Acknowledgment of Appoint by Agent**, **(02)** **Acknowledgment of Resignation by Agent**, and **(03)** **Affidavit of Full Force and Effect**. The Principal's forms are as follows: **(01)** **Revocation in Whole**, **(02)** **Revocation in Part(s)**, and **(03)** **Revocation of Agent**.

**Forms Miscellaneous:** These forms are available for the Principal; however, they are optional. Each document can stand alone and be extremely useful; think of it as an administrative support document that will make the Agent's life easier. These forms are as follows: **(01)** **Statement of Wishes**, **(02)** **Personal Information Worksheet**, **(03)** **Notification / Contact List**, **(04)** **Personal Documents Locator**, and **(05)** **Legal Document Locator**.

**Forms Recommended:** These forms are available for the Principal; however, they are optional. Each document can stand alone and be extremely useful; think of it as an administrative support document that will make the Agent's life easier. These forms are **(01)** **Affidavit of Principal's Health State** and **(02)** **Assets & Liabilities Worksheet**.

**Appendices:** These appendices are available for the Principal; however, these documents are optional (may be required). Each appendix can stand alone and be extremely useful; think of it as an administrative support document that will make the Agent's life easier. These appendices are as follows: **(01)** **Appendix A: Insurance Suggestions & Resource Guide**, **(02)** **Appendix B: Directions for Prudent & Safe Investing**, **(03)** **Appendix C: Attorney Suggestions & Resource Guide**, and **(04)** **Appendix D: Steps for Credit Repair & Statute of Limitations**.

# PUBLICATIONS

## PAQUETTE

"Whoever is trying to bring you down is already below you." ~ Ziad K. Abdelnou

# Be Pragmatic - Not Idealistic

The Principal should take great stride in being practical, especially regarding the nature of Power, Money, Time Management, and Motivation. Just because the Principal writes down what they want an Agent to do and bestows power to an Agent does not mean that the Principal's objectives will occur. For the Principal's objective to become a reality, there must be proper incentives or a great underlying sense of duty and honor. The Principal should read the topics below and evaluate their estate-planning situation realistically. Failure to do so otherwise will result in disaster.

**Communication:** Before drafting a Power of Attorney (**POA**), the Principal should take the time and make a phone call to the potential Agent(s) to verify if the Agent(s) are willing to act on the Principal behalf in a fiduciary manner. **Rhetorical Questions:** What is the point of appointing an Agent in a POA if the Agent declines to act later?

**Administrative:** When implementing a POA, make sure that all Agent(s) have an Original Notarized POA for their personal use in their possession. Failure to provide each Agent(s) with an Original Notarized POA will prevent or hinder their ability to execute the Principal's goals, objectives, and wishes. If the Agent(s) is completely unaware of the Principal's POA existence, do not expect anything to occur. A POA is useless if placed in a dresser drawer; remember to give the POA to the Agent(s).

Most businesses and institutions want to see the original notarized POA before letting the Agent(s) act for the Principal. The business or institution will usually make a copy of the original notarized POA for their file.

**Transparency:** Transparency begins with the Principal. If the Principal only provides POA to one of the Agents but not the others, it is foolhardy to expect an Agent to make copies and inform other Agent(s) and Third Parties of the Principal's POA.

Knowledge is power; an Agent will most likely not inform other legitimate Third Parties of the limits of their power. Thus, transparency is paramount to equalize the knowledge deficit that may exist and prevent such abuse of power.

**Financial Resources:** Do not expect an Agent(s) to perform out of the kindness of their heart and from their pockets. Be prepared to monetary reimburse the Agent(s) for their time and effort.

If the Principal wants specific actions to occur, ensure financial resources are available to achieve those objectives. Do not expect the Agent(s) to finance and pay for the Principal's objectives and wishes.

**Write Clearly:** When writing provisions and directives within the POA, the Principal must accomplish the following:
**(01)** The Principal must write clearly, as to what the Principal wants the Agent(s) to achieve;
**(02)** The Principal must not be vague, inconsistent, or conflicting about their intent and desires.

# PUBLICATIONS

## PAQUETTE

"Challenges are what make life interesting and overcoming them is what make life meaningful." ~ Joshua J. Marine

## To Joel A. Robertson

You are a true friend, a true blessing in my life.

# Table of Contents

Image Source – Art, Graphics, Illustrations, Photos
Types of POA – Explanation of the different kinds of POA
Power of Attorney – Current & Future Books by the Author
Declaration – Current & Future Books by the Author
Advance Directives – Current & Future Books by the Author
Relationship Agreements – Current & Future Books by the Author
Technical Support – Word Programs, PDF Editors, and Printers
Downloadable Digital Files – PDF, DOCX, DOC, ODT
CD / DVD – Page allocated for Sleeve & CD / DVD

This page is
intentionally
left blank

# CHAPTER 01

# Introductions

# CHAPTER 01

## Overview

# Introductions

## Overview

Chapter 01 provides the opportunity for the Author to communicate directly with the Reader (Purchaser or User) regarding the purpose and goals of this book. Furthermore, the Author briefly comments on the positive and negative attributes that the Reader (Purchaser or User) may encounter when using a self-help law book (Growing Trends, Cost/Value Analysis, Local Rules, Law Dynamics, and Legal Research).

- **Purpose of this Book**                    **(0.4 Pages Total)**
  Self-explanatory - outlines the author's primary motivation and answers the "why" question.

- **Goal of this Book**                        **(0.2 Pages Total)**
  Self-explanatory - outlines the author's goal and states what the author is trying to achieve.

- **Using Self – Help Law Books**              **(0.1 Pages Total)**
  Highlights the advantages and disadvantages of doing one's legal work and expands on the topic below to include the following: Growing Trend, Cost / Value Analysis, Local Rules, and Changes in the Law.

- **Growing Trends**                           **(0.3 Pages Total)**
  The author's commentary explains why doing one's legal work has become a growing trend in today's society.

- **Cost / Value Analysis**                    **(0.4 Pages Total)**
  The author's commentary explains the economic benefits and value of doing one's legal work.

- **Local Rules**                              **(0.2 Pages Total)**
  The author's commentary explains how local rules can potentially affect a legal document's execution and legitimacy.

- **Law Dynamics**                             **(0.2 Pages Total)**
  The author's commentary explains how laws serve society and how the evolution of laws reflects society's needs.

- **Legal Research**                           **(0.2 Pages Total)**
  The author's commentary explains how to perform and research legal issues using various methodologies.

# Purpose of this Book

In the Author's humble opinion and experience, most people need "living" legal documents that can adjust and "provide for breathing room" over time, with practical concepts and applications relevant to everyday life.

Through research and experience, the Author has analyzed numerous legal forms, with the majority sharing the following characteristics: (**01**) lack of detail and depth, (**02**) lack of options, and (**03**) very narrow in purpose or scope, especially when the subject matter is broad and vast. These deficiencies are primarily due to legal forms being locality or state-specific, usually deriving from the statutory form that had to meet the approval of some committee in which agendas (political, religious, and lobbyist) dictate available options. These statutory forms typically give a courteous overview of the subject matter in question without addressing the finer details and permeable conditions that one usually encounters in life. The lack of personal rights and liberties offer in statutory forms leaves little in the way of protection.

When Attorneys draft legal forms, these forms are usually premade with boilerplate language. Unless the client explicitly asks the Attorney to include specifics to address the eventualities that may occur with protective language in a disaster, said safety features are invisible. The lack of protectionism and detail is primarily due to the Attorney's inherent conflict of getting the job done in the least amount of time possible to maximize profits. Conversely, a client is usually unwilling to pay a high legal fee to compensate the Attorney for the time necessary to make said legal document "Iron Clad." A financial equilibrium develops when drafting a legal document with the unspoken agreement of "hey, this may not work in all life situations." Thus, the client may have to consult with an Attorney yet again and spend more money if an unanticipated situation occurs.

Power of Attorney is the focus of this book; within this book is (**01**) one Simple Power of Attorney (**Limited**). This Power of Attorney has an estate planning focus that provides options, depth, and flexibility while maintaining uniformity with built-in and optional (Durability Provisions) safety features.

# The Goal of this Book

The goal of the Author through this book is to provide legal forms with an estate planning focus that has options and depth while maintaining uniformity, thus offering clear directives that are flexible with built-in safety features that are inherently lacking in most legal forms.

The design of these legal forms within this book is for use in the United States of America. Use these legal forms as a template and adjust them appropriately with the help of a competent, licensed Attorney if the Purchaser or User lives in another country. These legal forms may be most applicable and adaptable to countries with a legal basis derived from Great Britain's common law approach; thus, any of Great Britain's current and former colonies are good candidates. Remember, laws from various countries differ; however, laws tend to converge to form some universal doctrine; this phenomenon has increased rapidly due to technological advancement, thus allowing for the greater exchange of ideas. **Please Note:** Not all countries are at the same convergence rate; countries with similar roots and thoughts will be closer to convergence. The disparity can be significant, especially regarding laws from two distinct and separate cultures.

The Author hopes that the goals stated in this book succeed or surpass the Purchaser's or User's expectations and give the Purchaser or User a sense of peace and security in their everyday life.

# Using Self-Help Law Books

One should be aware of the inherent advantages and disadvantages of doing one's legal work. Thus, it behooves the Purchaser or User to understand the challenges and difficulties this may encompass. The Author will briefly discuss the following: Growing Trends, Cost/Value Analysis, Local Rules, Law Dynamics, and Legal Research when using self-help law books.

# • Growing Trends

There has been a noticeable trend for Purchasers or Users to prepare their legal documents and handle their legal affairs versus hiring an Attorney. Courts across this country recognize that legal services are expensive and make every effort to make it easier for the individual(s) to represent themselves. However, on the reverse side of the coin, do not expect the courts to accommodate and provide sympathy for Purchaser or User who chooses not to utilize an Attorney. Some legal professionals and courts take the attitude, "want to save a buck, fine; however, if the Purchaser or User has any questions, go to the law library and figure it out."

The Author believes the Purchaser or User should have options, to make their lives easier and less confusing from a legal perspective. The Author tries to make these forms modular, universal, and easy to understand, with built-in directions. However, the Author cannot cover every conceivable possibility and include all the nuances due to local laws, statutes, and ruling. Thus, it is highly advantageous that the Purchaser or User seeks the advice of a competent, licensed State Attorney if clarification or additional help regarding legal issues is required.

# • Cost / Value Analysis

The global marketplace offers many options when shopping for a product or service with various quality levels and price points. When deciding on purchasing a product or service, the Purchaser or User will internally make a cost/value analysis base on their willingness to pay for the desired quality.

Most legal situations are straightforward and require a simple form, no complex analysis, some intelligence, and the ability to follow instructions. In situations like these, it makes sense to do one's legal work to save money at the expense of a small amount of the Purchaser's or User's time. However, in special or unique situations that are incredibly complex, a personal approach is prudent; seek a licensed attorney who can provide such service. Do not be cheap, realize one's limitations, and admit when help is required.

Creating a self-help law book involving legal matters entails simplifying the laws and condensing several legal cases into a single sentence or paragraph. Due to such simplifications, complications may arise that only an Attorney will notice. Remember, this is not a law book; if it were, it would be about a thousand pages long and too complex for most people to understand. The simplification process does entail leaving out many details and nuances that may apply to unique or unusual situations. Depending on whose opinion and specialty, there may be several valid interpretations for a legal principle or basis; thus, the possibility exists that a Judge may disagree with the Author's analysis.

Therefore, when deciding to utilize a self-help law book and do one own legal work, a cost/value analysis occurs. The Purchaser or User has to decide to save money (money spent on an Attorney instead) by doing the legal work themself, thus calculating that their efforts will outweigh the chances of rejection for their case (legal matters). Most individuals deciding to handle their legal affairs never encounter a legal problem, but occasionally people find that it costs more to have an Attorney fix their problem than to hire an Attorney to deal with it in the beginning. The Author is not trying to dissuade the Purchaser or User from legal empowerment but only to disclose the risk when handling one's legal matters. Consult with a competent, licensed State Attorney if the Purchaser or User has any questions or needs guidance.

# • Local Rules

This book is not all-inclusive; there are limitations regarding what a self-help law book can do for the Purchaser or User. One should be aware that there are bound to be procedural differences that vary from state to state, county to county, and potentially even Judge to Judge. The Purchaser or User should not expect to be able to get all the information and resources solely from within the confines of this book or any book. However, this book will serve as a guide to give the Purchaser or User-specific information whenever possible to help find out what else the Purchaser or User may need to know.

It is highly advantageous that before using any of the forms within this book, the Purchaser or User consults with their court clerk. The court clerks will inform the Purchaser or User if there are any local rules or forms that one should be aware of that are required. Usually, these forms will require the same information as the forms within this book but merely format differently, with slightly different wording, or using different color paper so that the clerk can quickly locate the document. The court clerk may ask for additional information to process the legal document.

# • Law Dynamics

The law is not static and constant; it is ever-evolving and dynamic. Given enough time, social and political pressures will change the laws, thus reflecting the very fabric of our civilization, as age-old rulings are overturned and lie fallow. This book is not a reflection pool, nor is the Author a seer who can peer into the future. It behooves the Purchaser or User of this book to check for the most recent statutes, rules, and regulations to see if any changes have occurred since its publication.

In most cases, the changes in the law will be insignificant, for example, a redesigned form, extra information, or alteration to a waiting period. Thus, the Purchaser or User might need to revise a form, file another form, or wait for an additional time; these changes will not usually affect the outcome of a case / legal matter. However, significant changes occasionally happen, and the entire law in a particular area requires a new interpretation. A legal case that serves as the basis for a central legal point becomes invalid, null, or void, thus impairing the Purchaser's or User's legal goal. If there are unique local requirements or recent changes in the law, seek the advice of a competent, licensed Attorney.

# • Legal Research

If the Purchaser or User needs additional information, consult the local law library, usually found at the county courthouse or a law school. Ask the librarian for assistance concerning the subject matter of interest. The primary source of information will be in the State's Statutes or Codes, with titles such as "Revised" or "Annotated" the title may include the publisher's name, and there could be more than one publisher. Ensure the Purchaser or User has the current version of their State laws. The most common way to update law books is a soft-cover supplement found on the back of each volume; other methods include supplement volume, loose-leaf bindings, and supplement sections. An additional source of legal information is as follows: Internet Research (suggests visiting **www.findlaw.com**); Practice manuals; Digest (gives summaries of appeals court cases); Case Reporter (contains full written opinions of appeals court cases); and Legal Encyclopedia (Major sets include *American Jurisprudence* and *Corpus Juris Secundum*).

# CHAPTER 02

# Instructions

# CHAPTER 02

## Overview

# Instructions

## Overview

The following are stand-alone instructional pages for convenience purposes only; each document within this chapter comes with built-in instructions for easy completion. These stand-alone instructional pages may help clarify questions or provide additional insights that the Reader (Purchaser or User) may have.

- ## POA's Legal Requirement                (01 Pages Total)
  The author explains the legal requirements, justifications, and prudent measures for the Principal, Witnesses, and Notary within the United States of America.

- ## Instructions for Principal                (01 Pages Total)
  This (stand-alone) instructional page guides the Principal as to what their requirements are when it comes to filling out a Power of Attorney (Simple, Complex, Durable, and Special) within this book.

- ## Instructions for Witnesses                (01 Pages Total)
  This (stand-alone) instructional page guides the Witnesses as to what their requirements are when it comes to filling out a Power of Attorney (Simple, Complex, Durable, and Special) within this book.

- ## Instructions for Notary Public                (01 Pages Total)
  This (stand-alone) instructional page guides the Notary Public as to what their requirements are when it comes to filling out a Power of Attorney (Simple, Complex, Durable, and Special) and Supporting Documents within this book.

- ## Built-In Safety Features                (06 Pages Total)
  These (stand-alone) instructional pages highlight the Built-in Safety Feature found in the Power of Attorney (Simple, Complex, Durable, and Special) within this book.

- ## Optional Safety Features                (01 Pages Total)
  These (stand-alone) instructional pages highlight the Optional Safety Feature found predominately in this book's Power of Attorney (Simple and Special).

# POA's Legal Requirements

## Not A Court Order:

A Power of Attorney (**POA**) is not a court order; the execution of this POA is strictly voluntary; implementation of the POA **must be proactive to be effective and valid**. Falsification of this POA may constitute a criminal offense.

## Recordation:

It is highly advantageous (more acceptable to bank officials or other financial institutions) that the Principal record/file (usually optional) the POA with the courts/official state record keeper, usually at the county level known as "county recorder of deeds." Utilizing a POA for Real Estate Transactions will require recordation and a Thumb/Finger Print in the Execution and Signature Page. It is advisable to consult with a licensed Attorney or the County Recorder of Deeds if there are any special filing/recording requirements.

## Various State Laws:

As of 2011, every State within the U.S.A. has enacted the Uniform Power of Attorney Act (UPOAA) except for Louisiana; however, each State may have differences concerning the legal requirements relating to the execution of a POA. All States require that the Principal (the person enacting the POA) sign and date the POA. Depending upon the State, the requirements for Witnesses are the following: (**01**) one or more Witnesses, (**02**) two Witnesses and a Notary Public, or (**03**) either two Witnesses or a Notary Public. In States where both a Witnesses and a Notary Public are requirements, some States require notarization of only the Principal's signature. In contrast, other states require notarization of the Principal and both Witnesses. Free notary services are usually within a Government Facility, Post Office, or Public Libraries.

## Legal Prudence:

Due to the various legal requirements of each State, the POA within this book conforms to the most prudent of measures concerning Principal, Witnesses, and Notary Public requirements. Thus, every POA within this book requires the Principal Signature and Date, (**02**) two Witnesses Signature and Date, and a Notary Public attestation to the Principal and Witnesses Signature and Date, along with the Notary Public's Seal, Signature, and Date. By notarizing the POA, the Principal has made it extremely difficult for a Third Party to challenge the validity of the Principal's signature and intentions.

## Principal Requirements:

Although not all states require the following concerning the Principal, it is a prudent practice that the Principal meets the following criteria to execute a POA (to prevent future legal challenges). (**01**) The Principal is at least eighteen (**18**) years or older. (**02**) The Principal is of sound and disposing mind (emotionally and mentally competent). (**03**) The Principal has the capacity with full memory or necessary mental faculties. (**04**) The Principal willfully and voluntarily executes this POA. **Please Note:** If the Principal is old and may exhibit signs of functioning non-socially, incapacitated, or incompetent in the future, it is highly advantageous that the Principal proactively implements an **Affidavit of Principal's Health State** before implementing a POA.

## Witnesses and Notary Public Requirements:

Although not all states require the following concerning the Witnesses and Notary Public, it is a prudent practice that the Witnesses and Notary Public do not have a conflict of interest and thus be impartial during the execution process of the POA (this is to prevent future legal challenges). These criteria will be grounds for a conflict of interest if the Witnesses or Notary Public is one or more: (**01**) Any individual related to the Principal by blood, marriage, or adoption. (**02**) Any individual who is currently a Beneficiary of the Principal's estate (laws of intestate succession or any existing will/codicil). (**03**) Any individual who benefits from a financial policy (insurance or annuity), in which the Principal's life is the insured. (**04**) Any individual claiming (present/inchoate) any portion of the Principal's estate. (**05**) Any individual who serves as an Owner, Operator, or employee of a Health Care Facility (Medical, Mental, Assisted Living), in which the Principal is currently a Patient / Client unless the employee serves solely as a Notary Public. (**06**) Any Doctor, Physician, Psychologist, Psychiatrist, Social Worker, Financial Advisor, and Financial Manager in which the Principal is currently a Patient / Client. (**07**) Any individual who serves as an Owner, Operator, or employee of a Final Dispositional Facility (Funerary Home, Crematory Authority, and Cemetery Authority) unless the employee serves solely as a Notary Public. (**08**) Any individual who is an Agent (active/inactive) serving in a fiduciary capacity under this POA. (**09**) Upon the Principal death, any individuals or entities may have a claim (the creditor) against the Principal's estate. (**10**) Any individual under the age of eighteen (**18**) years or is currently incapacitated or incompetent. The Witnesses should be twenty-one (**21**) years of age or older.

## Benefits:

The above requirements may seem burdensome and overzealous on the Author's part to impose upon the Principal, especially if the State of residency does not require all of these extra precautions; however, the end benefits are well worth it. By enacting these prudent measures concerning the Principal, Witnesses, and Notary --- companies, third-party service providers, and professionals (Doctors, Attorneys, Financial Advisers, et cetera) are more likely to honor the POA without questions. If the invocation of the POA was to occur in another State, the Principal could rest peacefully knowing that their POA would be just as effective and legitimate in that State.

## Revocation:

When revoking a POA, two (**02**) Witnesses and a Notary Public are preferred; however, a Notary Public is a bare minimum requirement. Furthermore, a current **Affidavit of Principal's Health State** accompanying the Revocation is highly advantageous, especially if legally challenged in the future. All Revocation documents within this book require notarization.

**Instructions**

© 2018 by Paul M. Paquette; Form v3.00
All Rights Reserved; Paquette Publications

Power of
Attorney

Must verify Agent Identity with
a Government Issue Picture I.D.

Page 01 of 01

# Instructions for Principal

A Principal is a person who implements (fills out and executes) a legal document (Power of Attorney) that gives power to another person named the Agent to interact with and create a legal arrangement with a Third Party.

**Fill out the Identifying Information of the Key Individual (Principal, Agent, Protector):**

**Key Individual →**

Full Name:
Address:
Phone #: Email:
Residence: County: State:

The following are selection choices in various formats that the Principal will encounter throughout the Power of Attorney.

"Y" or "N" Here ↑   Initial Here ↑

Place "Y" for Yes or "N" for No in the box and initial "✎" the line if the Principal desires the following:

**(A)   Effective Immediately**

Place a "✓" in the box if the Principal desires the following:

**Report Period:** [ ] None [ ] Monthly [ ] Quarterly [ ] Annually

The Principal wants to establish an expiration date for this POA as stated below:

**The date that POA Expires:** Month of: _____ Day of: _____ Year of: _____

**Fill out the Identifying Information of the Principal as shown in Signature and Execution:**

**Principal →**

Full Legal Name:

Today's Date:

Signature: ✎

Thumb/Finger Print:

Real Estate Transaction

**Optional Safety Feature**: At the bottom of **each** page of the Legal document is a security device reference as the Security Footer; if the **Security Footer** setting is to "**Low**," "**Moderate**," or "**High**," then the **Principal** needs to initial the bottom of each page as designated below for that page to be valid and enforceable.

1st Witness: _____ 2nd Witness: _____ Notary Public: _____ Principal: _____

# Instructions for Witnesses

A Witness(es) is a person(s) who signs their name to the legal documents for attestation purposes concerning the authenticity that the Principal has authorized a course of action.

The role of the Witness is to verify that the Principle is 18 years of age or older, has created said legal document, and did so of their free choice while in a state of mental and emotional competency. When selecting a witness, the criteria are as follows: 18 years or older (prefer 21 years), cannot benefit directly or indirectly from the Principal, unbiased party, and no immediate relation to the Principal. On the **Signature and Execution Page** is the following regarding the (02) two Qualified Adult Witnesses.

**Have (02) two Adult Witness\* the Principal's signature in addition to having their signature notarized\***

In the joint presence of each other, the Witnesses State that the Principal is the following: (**01**) The Principal is at least eighteen (**18**) years or older. (**02**) The Principal is of sound and disposing mind (emotionally and mentally competent). (**03**) The Principal is not suffering from constraint, duress, fraud, or undue influence. (**04**) The Principal acknowledges having willfully and voluntarily dated and signed this POA (or asked/directed for such actions to occur). (**05**) The Witnesses affirm that they have no direct biological or marital relationship with the Principal and are not a Beneficiary of the Principal's estate. (**06**) The Witnesses affirm their impartiality and confirm that the criterion stated in the box at the bottom of the last page does not apply. (**07**) The Witnesses declare this paragraph true and correct under the Penalty of Perjury.

**If the Witness is uncomfortable giving out personal contact information, current employment information and occupation will suffice.**

| 1st Witness → | Name: | | Signature: |
|---|---|---|---|
| | Address: | | |
| | Phone #: | | Date: |
| | Occupation: | | |

| 2nd Witness Or Special Witness \*\* → | Name: | | Signature: |
|---|---|---|---|
| | Address: | | |
| | Phone #: | | Date: |
| | Occupation: | | |

**Optional Safety Feature**: At the bottom of **each** page of the Legal document is a security device reference as the Security Footer; if the **Security Footer** setting is "**High**," then the two (**02**) **Witness** need to initial the bottom of each page as designated below for that page to be valid and enforceable.

1st Witness: _____    2nd Witness: _____    Notary Public: _____    Principal: _____

# Instructions for Notary Public

A Notary Public is a public officer constituted by law to serve the public in non-contentious matters. Whose primary functions are to (**01**) administer oaths/affirmations and (**02**) witness and authenticate the executions of the legal documents.

The Notary Public's role is to verify that the Principle is 18 years of age or older, has created said legal document, and did so of their free choice while in a state of mental and emotional competency. Furthermore, the Notary Public shall attest that witnesses have signed this document in their presence. When selecting a Notary Public, the criteria are as follows: 18 years or older (prefer 21 years), cannot benefit directly or indirectly from the Principal, unbiased party, and no immediate relation to the Principal. On the **Signature and Execution Page** is the following that relates to the Notary Public.

**UNDER THE LAWS OF →**

COUNTY: _____

STATE: _____

Before the Notary Public (the undersigned authority) comes forth, the Principal, with a sound/disposed mind, is eighteen (**18**) years or older. The Principal acknowledges having willfully and voluntarily dated and signed this POA (or asked/directed for such actions to occur) stated above in the Notary Public presence. If Witnesses sign and attest that the Principal has signed this POA, the Notary Public shall attest that the Witnesses have signed this POA in the Notary Public's presence. Furthermore, the Notary Public states that the Principal has provided a Government Issue identification card with a facial picture to prove identity. The Notary Public declares under the Penalty of Perjury that this paragraph is true and correct.

**If the Principal or Witnesses sign this POA but not in the presence of the Notary Public, then the Notary Public will not notarize or sign this POA.**

**\* Notary Public →**

Full Name: _____   **Signature & Seal:** _____

Location: _____

Address: _____

Phone #: _____   I.D. Number: _____

Date: _____   Commission Expires: _____

**Optional Safety Feature**: At the bottom of **each** page of the Legal document is a security device reference as the Security Footer; if the **Security Footer** setting is **Moderate**" or "**High**," then the **Notary Public** needs to initial the bottom of each page as designated below for that page to be valid and enforceable.

1st Witness: _____ 2nd Witness: _____ Notary Public: _____ Principal: _____

**Built-In Safety Features**

# Built-in Safety Features

These documents come with **Built-in Safety Features** to protect the Principal; the following examples illustrate these safety features and explain why they exist.

**Choice Selection:** It allows the Principal to select "**Yes**" or "**No**" with either a **Y** or **N**; along with initialization, this allows for modulation and verification for choice selection.

## Article III: Effective Date of POA

The Principal wants the following regarding the effective date for the legal enforcement of this POA: The Principal can choose from (**02**) two options; however, **options A** and **B** are mutually exclusive. **Option A** shall be the default option in the event of ambiguities.

Place "**Y**" for Yes or "**N**" for No in the box and initial "✎" the line if the Principal desires the following:

**(A)** | **Effective Immediately**

"Y" or "N" Here ↑    Initial Here ↑

By designating "**Y**" for Yes, the effective date of this POA shall begin from the day of execution, as stated in **Article XXI**. If durability provision(s) are active in **Article XIV**, those provision(s) shall immediately take effect.

Place "**Y**" for Yes or "**N**" for No in the box and initial "✎" the line if the Principal desires the following:

**(B)** | **Effective if Events are Trigger**

"Y" or "N" Here ↑    Initial Here ↑

By designating "**Y**" for Yes, the effective date of this POA shall begin when such events transpire or occur, as outlined in **Article V: "Springing Powers."** If durability provision(s) are active in **Article XIV**, the durability provision(s) shall be active when such events transpire, as outlined in **Article V: "Springing Powers."**

**Agent Conflict of Interest**: This Safety feature protects the Principal from conflict of interest and situations where the Principal's financial interest may be at stake.

## Article VII: Designation of Agent

The Principal should only designate an Agent if that individual is **Reliable**, **Trustworthy**, and **Competent** to manage the Principal's affairs. For legal reasons, all Agents must be competent and at least eighteen (**18**) years or older. None of the following individuals (non-relative) may serve as the Principal's Agent. (**A**) Any individual who serves as an Owner, Operator, or employee of a Health Care Facility (Medical, Mental, or Assisted Living) in which the Principal is currently a Patient / Client unless the employee serves solely as a Notary Public. (**B**) Any individual who serves as an Owner, Operator, or employee of a Final Dispositional Facility (Funerary Home, Crematory Authority, and Cemetery Authority) unless the employee serves solely as a Notary Public. (**C**) Any Doctor, Physician, Psychologist, Psychiatrist, Social Worker, Financial Advisor, or Financial Manager in which the Principal is currently a Patient / Client. Automatic Revocation of the Spouse designation as Agent shall occur if the following happens: (**01**) Dissolution or annulment of the marriage. (**02**) Proceedings are currently active for Dissolution of Marriage. (**03**) The Principal currently lives in a separate physical location from their Spouse for more than (**02**) two months with the intention of a divorce. The Principal designates the following individual as the Agent, the first choice, with decision-making powers in adherence to the terms and conditions specified in this POA.

# Built-in Safety Features

These documents come with **Built-in Safety Features** to protect the Principal; the following examples illustrate these safety features and explain why they exist.

**Yellow Space**: This Safety feature ensures that the Principal can write in additional directions or terms (conditions, prohibitions, restrictions, exceptions, additions, limitations, extensions, and special rules). Option One (**01**) requires the writing to be " **Type**." Option Two (**02**) requires the writing to be "**Type**" or "**Legible writing in Ink**" but not both.

**Option One (01):** / **Option Two (02):**

Specify in Detail — Must be Type

Specify in Detail — Preferably Type or Legible writing in Ink

**Restrictions on Agent's Power**: This Safety feature protects the Principal from actions that the Agent may do that are harmful to the Principal.

## Article X: Restrictions on Agent's Powers

**A:** Regardless of what authorization or powers bestow in **Article VII Subsection A through X,** the Agent shall not do or perform the following: **(01)** The Agent shall not make a loan to oneself, another name Agent, or a beneficiary of the Agent. **(02)** The Agent shall not take a service fee as an Agent. **(03)** The Agent shall not create, modify, or revoke a trust. **(04)** The Agent shall not use the Principal's property to fund a trust for someone other than the Principal or a trust that does not benefit the Principal greater than seventy (70%) percent. **(05)** The Agent shall not create or change a Beneficiary's interest in the Principal's property. **(06)** The Agent shall not create or change the Principal's interest in the Principal's property solely for the benefit of another. **(07)** The Agent shall not designate or change the designation of beneficiaries to receive any property, benefit, or contract right on the Principal's death. **(08)** The Agent shall not make or revoke a gift of the Principal property in trust or another arrangement. **(09)** The Agent shall not make or revoke a gift on the Principal behalf. **(10)** The Agent shall not exercise any powers that would cause the Principal's assets to become taxable to the Agent or the Agent's estate for any income, estate, or inheritance tax. **(11)** The Agent shall not forgive debts owed to the Principal, disclaim, or waive benefits payable to the Principal. **(12)** The Agent shall not execute, publish, declare, amend, or revoke the following: last will, codicil, or any will substitute on the Principal's behalf. **(13)** The Agent shall not perform duties under a contract that requires the Principal's services. **(14)** The Agent shall not make an affidavit about the Principal's knowledge that is unknown to the Agent personally. **(15)** The Agent shall not vote in any governmental public election on behalf of the Principal unless the Agent has a notarized letter stating who the Principal's candidates and voting preferences are regarding that public election. **(16)** The Agent shall not exercise powers and authority granted to the Principal as Trustee or a court-appointed Fiduciary. **(17)** The Agent shall not exercise the right to make a disclaimer on behalf of the Principal, except for a disclaimer of a detrimental transfer or acceptance made with the court's approval. **(18)** The Agent shall not enjoin (add or transfer) ownership or title to the Principal's funds or assets in the Agent's name alone. **Please Note:** Waiver of these restrictions shall only occur if the Principal grants written permission in **Article IX Subsection Y.**

# Built-in Safety Features

These documents come with **Built-in Safety Features** to protect the Principal; the following examples illustrate these safety features and explain why they exist.

**Additional Legal Provisions:**  These safety features protect the Principal.

**Modifications:**  Ensure the document's legitimacy and integrity.

**N:  Modification:** Changes or modifications to this POA shall not occur upon execution. If the Principal wants to change this POA, the Principal must make an entirely new one. However, revocation of any part(s) of this POA may occur if it is in writing; once a part(s) receives revocation, it shall be permanent.  Alterations (strikes out, cross out, and blackouts) of any provisions or writing within this POA shall have no bearing in a court of law and shall remain active and valid as to their original intent.

**Picture I.D.:**  Ensure the legitimacy of the Agent.

**O:  Picture I.D.:** The Principal requires verifying the Agent's identity with a government-issued picture ID. The Principal does not require it to be current and up to date; all that the Principal requires is the ability to confirm their facial features in a picture from an official governmental source.

**Governing Law**: Determines which laws and jurisdiction shall take priority if a legal issue arises.

**T:  Governing Law:** This POA shall take effect immediately as a sealed instrument and shall receive interpretation, enforcement, and governance under the State's laws where the Principal has established physical residency at the time of enforcement. The Principal requests for the honoring of this POA in any State, County, or Location in which the Principal's body or property may be, with the intention that it be valid in all jurisdictions/territories of the United States and all Foreign Nations. This POA is to receive the most liberal interpretation available to grant the appointed Fiduciary the greatest amount of decision-making discretion.

**Severability / Saving Clause:** This clause ensures the survival and permanency of the legal document if certain sections or provisions are illegal or invalid.

**U:  Severability / Saving Clause:** An invalid or unenforceable provision within this POA might exist. If that occurs, the remaining provisions of this POA shall continue and be active as if said invalid or unenforceable provision did not exist. All remaining provisions shall be undisturbed to maintain their original legal meaning, force, and effect. If a court finds or deems that an invalidated or unenforceable provision will become valid if limitations exist, then such written provision shall receive a written modification by court order to limit the provision's power while maximizing the economic value and liberties granted.

**Court Appointed of Guardian or Conservator:** The Principal can nominate an individual in advance if the Courts decide upon a Guardian or Conservator.

**X:  Court Appointed Guardian or Conservator:** the Principal intends by this POA to avoid a court-supervised guardianship or conservatorship. If the Principal attempts or fails to avoid a court-supervised guardianship or conservatorship. Then, the Principal requests that the Agent designated in this POA serve as Guardian or Conservator of the Principal's property and affairs.  The court-appointed Guardian or Conservator shall not have the power to revoke, suspend, or terminate this POA or the Agent's powers except as specifically authorized by law. The Principal may execute the following: **"Declaration in Advance of Need for Guardianship & Conservatorship,"** if execution occurs, the Principal prefers that those individuals act in such a fiduciary capacity.

# Built-in Safety Features

These documents come with **Built-in Safety Features** to protect the Principal; the following examples illustrate these safety features and explain why they exist.

**Acknowledgment by the Agent:** A basic overview of the Agent's Responsibility; this is to prevent the Agent from using the excuse "I did not know" and so forth. Furthermore, since this Acknowledgment is in the Power of Attorney, the Agent cannot claim ignorance regarding their fiduciary duties.

## Article XV: Acknowledgment by the Agent

**A:** The Agent shall exercise due care and act in the Principal's best interest with the powers granted while adhering to any limitations, impositions, or specifications within this POA.

**B:** The Agent's foremost duty is loyalty and protection of the Principal and the Principal's interests. The Agent shall direct any benefits derived from this POA to the Principal. The Agent must avoid conflicts of interest and use ordinary skill and prudence to exercise these powers. If there is anything about this POA or the Agent's duties that the Agent does not understand, the Agent shall seek professional advice.

**C:** A court of competent jurisdiction has the discretion to revoke the Agent's power, especially if acting inappropriately. Thus, it behooves the Agent to exercise the bestowed powers in a fiduciary manner. The burden will be upon the Agent to prove that such acts were prudent and within a Fiduciary standard for any questionable acts. The Agent may be liable for damages and subject to criminal and civil prosecution if a court of competent jurisdiction finds that the Agent has violated their fiduciary duty.

**D:** The Agent has the power to abstain from using their granted powers under this POA; however, the Agent does not have the luxury of being negligent when the **Life, Safety**, and **Welfare** of the Principal are at stake. The Agent may be liable for damages, be subject to prosecution (criminal or civil), and suffer termination of powers if a court rules that the Agent has been negligent regarding their fiduciary duty under this POA to the Principal,

**E:** The Agent agrees to keep all monetary funds or financial assets that belong to the Principal in separate accounts from the Agent's monetary funds or financial assets. There shall be no commingling of monetary funds or financial assets to ensure simple accounting and safeguard the Principal's financial security. Furthermore, the Agent agrees to protect, conserve, and exercise prudence and caution in dealings with the Principal's monetary funds, financial assets, and all other assets of value and worth.

**F:** The Agent agrees to keep a complete/accurate record of all acts, disbursements, and receipts for review/inspection. The Agent agrees to provide an accounting/report to the Principal at the following time intervals (as stated below). If the Principal dies, the Executor/Administrator of the Principal's estate shall receive the accounting/report within a quarter. **Directions: Place a "✓" in the Accounting / Report Period box.**

| Report Period: | | None | | Monthly | | Quarterly | | Annually |
|---|---|---|---|---|---|---|---|---|

**G:** By default, the Agent shall not receive compensation for their authority, rights, and responsibilities; however, the Agent may receive reimbursement for reasonable and necessary expenses incurred in performing their authority, rights, and responsibilities. The Principal may compensate the Agent if the Principal desires.

**H:** The Agent shall disclose all actions that require written authorization by using their identity as the Agent in the following manner: (Agent's Signature) as Agent for (Principal's Name).

**I:** For Simple and Special POA, the Agent may resign by notifying the Principal or the Principal's Guardian or Conservator (provided a Judge appoints one). For Complex and Durable POA, the Agent may resign by notifying the Principal, Protector, Co-Agent, Successor Agent, or the Principal's Guardian or Conservator (provided a Judge appoints one). The resignation must be in writing and sent by certified mail, statutory overnight delivery (return receipt requested), or email.

**J:** If the Agent becomes aware of the death of the Principal who executed the POA, the Agent must notify all Third Parties as soon as practicable that the Principal has died and that this POA is no longer legitimate and effective. If Durability Provision(s) are not active or applicable, the Agent must notify all Third Parties as soon as practicable that the Principal is functioning non-socially, incapacitated, or incompetent; thus, the POA is no longer valid.

**K:** If the Agent resigns or ceases to represent the Principal regarding this POA, the former Agent agrees to return all property and documents to the Principal immediately.

**Due to Space Limitations, Provisions L – R are not shown.**

# Built-in Safety Features

These documents come with **Built-in Safety Features** to protect the Principal; the following examples illustrate these safety features and explain why they exist.

**Interpretation Instruction in the event of Ambiguities:**   It provides a set of rules to avoid litigation and determine the Principal intent if an error occurs.

## Article XI: Ambiguities Interpretation Instructions

**A:** If a provision requires that a specific section be "Type" to be valid, failure to **"Type"** the section shall make that part invalid, null, and void.

**B:** If a provision requires that a specific section have the **Principal's Initial** for it to be valid, failure to initial the section shall make that part invalid, null, and void.

**C:** If a fillable section is **blank**, thus not typed or filled in, the legal interpretation shall be that the Principal did not intend for that section to be effective, and when it comes to interpreting that section, it shall be invalid, null, and void.

**D:** If a fillable section requires a **Yes "Y"** or **No "N"** and the section is blank (thus not typed or filled in), the legal interpretation shall be that the Principal did not intend for that section to be effective; therefore, it shall be **No "N."**

**E:** If a fillable section requires a **Yes "Y"** or **No "N;"** however, **"Yes"** or **"No"** exists instead, the legal interpretation shall be that the Principal did intend for that section to keep its legal effect and meaning.

**F:** If a fillable section requires a **Check "✓"** and it is blank, thus not typed or filled in, the legal interpretation shall be that the Principal did not intend for that section to be effective; therefore, not wanted.

**G:** If a fillable section gives multiple options that are mutually exclusive to each other in which a **Check "✓"** is required if more than one option is checked "✓" then the legal interpretation shall be that the Principal did this in error; thus when it comes to interpreting that section, the implementation shall be of the more conservative option.

**H:** If a fillable section requires a **Check "✓"** or "X," however a dash "—" exists instead, the legal interpretation shall be that the Principal did not intend for that section to be effective; thus, it is not wanted.

**I:** If a section or provision is typed with added handwritten instructions, only the "typed" section will receive consideration concerning the Principal's intentions. The rationale is simple: any person, not necessarily the Principal, can handwrite (ink in) after the fact. Due to a lack of verification, the additional handwritten instruction shall be invalid, null, and void.

**J:** Most state laws will void a legal document if someone writes on the surface, especially after notarization or execution. The Principal waives this right since the formalization of the POA requires it to be typed and printed; thus, any handwritten alteration concerning the altered section shall be unsubstantial and nonbearing unless an unaltered original duplicate or legitimate copy is available; only the unreadable section shall be invalid, null, and void,

**K:** If this POA allows handwritten statements by the Principal and there seem to be any suspicious alterations or additions (changes in handwriting style, changes in ink), such handwritten alterations or additions shall have no weight or bearing. Unless an unaltered original duplicate or legitimate copy is available, the altered section shall only be invalid, null, and void if it (the altered section) is unreadable as to its original intentions.

**L:** The Descriptions that follow a **Yes "Y"** or a **No "N"** Box are for clarification and informational purposes to outline the performance of duties and rights.

**M:** If a Third Party receives more than one active Power of Attorney regarding the Principal:  **(01)** The Power of Attorney that has the most recent date shall take more precedence unless otherwise stated in **Article VII Subsection G**. **(02)** If the Principal function non-socially, incapacitated, or incompetent, then the Power of Attorney that has an active Durability Provision(s), in effect, shall take precedence. **(03)** If the Power of Attorney has the same date, then a General Power takes precedence over a Financial Power of Attorney.  A Financial Power of Attorney takes precedence over a Banking Power of Attorney.  A Limited Power of Attorney shall be subservient to a General, Financial, and Banking Power of Attorney if any conflicts arise.  **(04)** A Protecting Power of Attorney shall stand alone and only be binding upon Complex and Durable Power of Attorney with active Protector provisions. **(05)** A Complex Power of Attorney takes precedence over a Simple Power of Attorney if any conflicts arise. **(06)** Unless otherwise specified within a Special Power of Attorney, a Special Power of Attorney shall take precedence over a Complex and Simple Power of Attorney if there are any conflicts.

# Built-in Safety Features

These documents come with **Built-in Safety Features** to protect the Principal; the following examples illustrate these safety features and explain why they exist.

**Witnesses and Notary Public Conflict of Interest:** This Safety feature protects the Principal from conflict of interest and situations where the Principal's financial interest may be at stake.

> **\* None shall serve as a Witness, Notary Public, or other qualified individual with the authority to administer oaths regarding this POA made under this section.**

**(01)** Any individual related to the Principal by blood, marriage, or adoption. **(02)** Any individual currently a Beneficiary of the Principal's estate (laws of intestate succession or any existing will/codicil). **(03)** Any individual who benefits from a financial policy (insurance or annuity) in which the Principal's life is insured. **(04)** Any individual claiming (present/inchoate) any part of the Principal's estate. **(05)** Any individual who serves as an Owner, Operator, or employee of a Health Care Facility (Medical, Mental, or Assisted Living) in which the Principal is currently a Patient / Client unless the employee serves solely as a Notary Public. **(06)** Any Doctor, Physician, Psychologist, Psychiatrist, Social Worker, Financial Advisor, or Financial Manager in which the Principal is currently a Patient / Client. **(07)** Any individual who serves as an Owner, Operator, or employee of a Final Dispositional Facility (Funerary Home, Crematory Authority, and Cemetery Authority) unless the employee serves solely as a Notary Public. **(08)** Any individual who is an Agent (active/inactive) serving in a fiduciary capacity under this POA. **(09)** Upon the Principal's death, any individual or entity with a claim (the creditor) against the Principal's estate. **(10)** Any individual under eighteen **(18)** years or is incapacitated or incompetent. The Witnesses should be twenty-one **(21)** years of age or older.

**Special Witness\*\*** If the Principal is a resident of a sanitarium, rest home, nursing home, boarding home, et cetera, it is highly beneficial that a patient advocate or ombudsman be one of the Witnesses while executing this POA.
**Legal Questions:** Consult the State laws or contact a licensed Attorney.

# This page is intentionally left blank

# Optional Safety Features

# Optional Safety Features

These documents come with **Optional Safety Features** to protect the Principal; the following example illustrates these safety features and explains why they exist.

**Durability Provisions:** This provision allows the Principal to "put in stone" per se the Agent's ability to continue to act on the Principal's behalf if the Principal were to suffer Incompetence, Incapacity, or Functioning Non-Socially in the future.

## Article XIII: Durability Provisions

**Statement of Understanding by the Principal:** The Principal understands that the direction and choices implemented by the Agent as specified in this POA (if still active due to durability provision(s) and not previously revoked) shall continue, even if the Principal objects to the actions or decisions later when the Principal is functioning non-socially, incapacitated, or incompetent.

**DIRECTIONS:** The Principal must **place "Y"** for **Yes** in all applicable empty box spaces below and initial "🖉" on **the line** for activation of Durable Power(s). The Principal must **place "N"** for **No** to all applicable empty box spaces below **and initial "🖉" the line** for no activation of Durable Power(s). Durable Power(s) will not receive activation if the empty box space or the Principal's initial is void or left blank.

| | | |
|---|---|---|
| "Y" or "N" Here ↑　　Initial Here ↑ | Place **"Y" for Yes or "N" for No** in the box and initial "🖉" the line if the Principal desires the following: | **(A)**　**Durability against Incompetence** |

**DESCRIPTION:** By designating "Y" for Yes, this POA shall continue if the Principal becomes incompetent; this POA shall survive the effects of incompetence and shall not be invalid, null, or void. Furthermore, the Agent's power and authority shall remain effective when the Principal is incompetent.

| | | |
|---|---|---|
| "Y" or "N" Here ↑　　Initial Here ↑ | Place **"Y" for Yes or "N" for No** in the box and initial "🖉" the line if the Principal desires the following: | **(B)**　**Durability against Incapacity** |

**DESCRIPTION:** By designating "Y" for Yes, this POA shall continue if the Principal becomes incapacitated; this POA shall survive the effects of incapacity and shall not be invalid, null, or void. Furthermore, the Agent's power and authority shall remain effective when the Principal is incapacitated.

| | | |
|---|---|---|
| "Y" or "N" Here ↑　　Initial Here ↑ | Place **"Y" for Yes or "N" for No** in the box and initial "🖉" the line if the Principal desires the following: | **(C)**　**Durability against Functioning Non-Socially** |

**DESCRIPTION:** By designating "Y" for Yes, this POA shall continue if the Principal functions Non-Socially; this POA shall survive the effects of functioning non-socially and shall not be invalid, null, or void. Furthermore, the Agent's power and authority shall remain effective when the Principal functions non-socially.

| | |
|---|---|
| **Recommendation:** | The Agent should attach the **Affidavit of Principal's Health State** by a licensed Health Professional (dated before the expiration date) if the Principal is functioning non-socially, incapacitated, or incompetent when presenting the POA to any Third Party. |

# CHAPTER 03

# Simple Limited Power of Attorney

# CHAPTER 03

## Overview

# Simple Limited Power of Attorney

## Overview

It is highly advantageous that the Principal trusts the person acting as their Agent completely for the Simple Limited Power of Attorney. That person shall have power over the Principal assets and affairs as if the Principal were there in person.

This Power of Attorney is "**Simple**" for the following reasons: (**01**) It names only one Agent with no successor Agent. (**02**) The effective date or expiration date is not contingent upon multiple variables. (**03**) There are no springing and sprinkling powers added. (**04**) Durable provision(s) are optional. (**05**) There are no other optional safety features available.

- ## Simple Limited Power of Attorney (SLPOA)            (14 Pages Total)

  Only utilize this document if necessary and in a prudent manner. This Power of Attorney gives the Agent limed powers (written by the Principal) and ability regarding the Principal's property and affairs. **Please Note:** If the Principal requires a Power of Attorney that covers Banking, Financial, or General Activities, the Principal will probably be better off choosing the Simple Banking Power of Attorney, Simple Financial Power of Attorney, or Simple General Power of Attorney.

# Simple Limited
# Power of Attorney

# Simple Limited Power of Attorney

## Objective:

The objective of this Simple Limited Power of Attorney (SLPOA) is to give the individual whom the Principal has designated as the Agent limited power (written by the Principal) and ability regarding the Principal's property and affairs. This Power of Attorney is Simple for the following reasons: **(01)** It names only one Agent with no successor Agent. **(02)** The effective or expiration date is not contingent upon multiple variables. **(03)** No springing and sprinkling powers were added. **(04)** Durable provision(s) are optional. **(05)** There are no other optional safety features available.

## Do The Following:

Please note that the possibility exists that transactions or third parties may not permit using this SLPOA; suggest checking for unusual requirements or imposition in advance. The Principal should know that most financial institutions or businesses would only honor a durable power of attorney. Usually, vetting of the power of attorneys must occur first in the legal department before utilization due to liability reasons. Upon filling out the SLPOA, print off at least **(03)** three copies, **(01)** one for each of the following: Principal, Agent, and each financial institution or business. Please note that the possibility exists that financial institutions or businesses will only honor a power of attorney of their own making; thus, the Agent may have to sue to enforce a power of attorney. Other financial institutions or businesses may have policies requiring the account holder to provide a power of attorney in person for their "folder" before utilization. Most financial institutions or businesses will not accept a Non-Durable Power of Attorney.

## Not A Court Order:

**Please Note:** This is not a court order. Executing this SLPOA is strictly voluntary. Implementing the SLPOA must be proactive to be effective and valid. It is highly advantageous that the Principal record/file (optional) the SLPOA with the courts or county clerk. Falsification of this SLPOA may constitute a criminal offense.

## Note of Caution:

When filling out this SLPOA, please consider the following. The Purchaser or User should seek a legal professional's advice if the Purchaser or User is less than eighteen (18) years of age and currently deemed mentally incompetent or incapacitated. Feel free to utilize this SLPOA as a template. However, without legal representation in the situation above, this SLPOA would suffer litigation by Interested Third Parties and more than likely receive judgment as invalid. Remember, an active lawful court order covering the subject matter within this SLPOA will always take precedence if a conflict occurs. **Please Note:** If the Purchaser or User does have an active court order. The Purchaser or User can design this SLPOA, so it is not in conflict; however, seek the advice of a legal professional if there are any questions.

# Simple Limited Power of Attorney

## Table of Contents:

## Helpful Suggestions / Recommendations:

- Most notaries who notarize a document for free as part of their occupation will usually only notarize one document versus having multiple originals. **Recommendation:** Find out what the Notary will do in advance.
- Keep the Original SLPOA in a safe place (preferably a fireproof vault or safe) and give an original copy to a trusted individual.
- Make multiple copies of this SLPOA. Give a copy to each interested Third Party. Maintain a list of who has copies of this SLPOA in their procession. Attach the list to the Original SLPOA in the Principal procession. If the SLPOA is revoked, refer to the list to retrieve the SLPOA in question.
- The easiest way to restrict this SLPOA is to establish an Expiration Date, preferably in five (**05**) to ten (**10**) year increments. Upon expiration of this SLPOA, the Principal will have to execute a new SLPOA to continue the agency relationship regarding the Principal's property and affairs.
- The Principal should execute an Affidavit of Principal's Health State by a licensed Health Professional if there are questions or doubts regarding the Principal's capacity, competence, or social functionality. Attach the executed Affidavit of Principal's Health State to the Original SLPOA. If applicable, give a trusted individual an original copy of the Affidavit of Principal's Health State.

# Simple Limited
# Power of Attorney

# Important Document

- Before signing this Simple Limited Power of Attorney (SLPOA), the Principal should know these important facts. This SLPOA aims to give the individual the Principal designates as their "Agent" **the limited power (written by the Principal) and ability regarding the Principal's property and affairs.**

- **Please Note:** While the Principal is competent, the Principal still has all the power and rights to control their property and affairs as the Principal deems fit, despite any powers the Principal may have bestowed.

- The Principal must talk to their Agent often, specifically about what the Agent does while using SLPOA. If the Agent is not following the Principal's written instructions, the Principal may revoke this SLPOA or end the Agent's powers.

- **Beware:** Please note that the possibility exists that Third Parties or certain transactions may not permit the use of this SLPOA; it is advisable to check in advance, if possible, for any special requirements or imposition.

- This SLPOA does not impose a duty on the Agent to exercise discretionary powers. However, when using these powers, the Agent must use due care to act for the Principal's benefit and adhere to this SLPOA. The Agent must act consistently with the Principal's desires, as stated in the SLPOA. Unless the Principal says or limits otherwise, the Agent has the same level of authority to make decisions. **Please Note:** A court could take away the powers of an Agent if the Agent authorizes anything that is illegal or acts contrary to this SLPOA.

- The Agent may exercise these powers throughout the Principal's lifetime unless otherwise limited in writing (time duration or event occurrence). Furthermore, these powers will continue to exist and shall be enforceable (if the durable provision(s) are active) if the Principal develops one or more of the following: **(01)** have a disability that renders the Principal to function non-socially. **(02)** The Principal is incapacitated. **(03)** The Principal is incompetent.

- This SLPOA does not authorize anyone to make health care decisions for the Principal. The Principal should implement the following if the Principal wishes to have health care decisions made: **(01)** Advanced Medical Health Directive, **(02)** Advanced Mental Health Directive, **(03)** Do Not Resuscitate Advance Directive (DNR), **(04)** Durable Power of Attorney for Health Care, **(05)** Declaration of Health Care (Living Will), and **(06)** Declaration of Organs & Tissues Donation (Anatomical Gifts).

- This SLPOA does not authorize anyone to decide guardianship regarding a minor or a disabled adult; neither gives the Agent the right to delegate Parental or Guardian authority. The Principal should implement the following if the Principal wishes to delegate their Parental / Guardian authority: **(01)** Simple or Complex Power of Attorney for Minor Child. **(02)** Durable Power of Attorney for Health Care of Minor Child. **(03)** Declaration of Guardianship & Conservatorship for Minor Child. **(04)** Declaration of Guardianship & Conservatorship for the Disabled.

- This SLPOA does not authorize anyone to decide guardianship or conservatorship regarding the Principal, nor does it give the Agent's powers of delegation regarding the Guardian or Conservator authority. If the Principal wishes to establish a Guardian or Conservator, the Principal should implement the following: **(01)** Declaration of Guardianship & Conservatorship.

- The creation and design of this SLPOA require no legal assistance to complete. The Principal or Agent should seek advice from a licensed Attorney for clarification or questions regarding this SLPOA.

- The Principal may revoke this SLPOA if the Principal is competent. The Principal should contact a licensed Attorney if the Agent continues to act after the Principal has revoked the Agent's powers and notified the Agent of their termination. Should the Principal revoke the Agent's authority, a written Revocation should be hand-delivered or mailed to where this SLPOA has been utilized.

- Use this SLPOA only after careful consideration. Execution and implementation by the Principals of this SLPOA should be free from pressure. Do not name an Agent or grant power unless it is the Principal's choice.

© 2018 by Paul M. Paquette; Form v3.00
All Rights Reserved; Paquette Publications

Simple Limited
Power of Attorney

You must verify the agent's identity
with a government-issued picture I.D.

Page 01 of 11

# Simple Limited Power of Attorney

## Article I: Creation Statement

The Principal (stated below) revokes every previous Simple Limited Power of Attorney with an execution date predating this document.

**Principal** →

| | |
|---|---|
| **Full Name:** | |
| **Address:** | |
| **Phone #:** | **Email:** |
| **Residence:** | **County:** **State:** |

The Principal affirms the following in the Witnesses and Notary presence: (**01**) The Principal is at least eighteen (**18**) years or older. (**02**) The Principal is of sound and disposing mind (emotionally and mentally competent) to make or request this Simple Limited Power of Attorney. (**03**) The Principal has the capacity with full memory or necessary mental faculties to understand and comprehend these actions. (**04**) The Principal willfully and voluntarily executes this Simple Limited Power of Attorney. The following abbreviations shall be used for brevity and consistency: Simple Limited Power of Attorney shall be "**SLPOA**," and Attorney-In-Fact shall be "**Agent**."

## Article II: Purpose

As stated in **Article V**, The Principal appoints, authorizes, and designates the following Agent to make decisions and perform actions for the Principal according to the SLPOA terms and conditions as indicated in **Article III** through **Article XIV**.

## Article III: Effective Date of SLPOA

The Principal wants the effective date of this SLPOA to begin on the day of execution, as stated in **Article XIV**. If durability provision(s) are active in **Article X**, those provision(s) shall immediately take effect.

## Article IV: Expiration Date of SLPOA

The Principal wants to establish an expiration date for this SLPOA as stated below:

**The date that SLPOA Expires:**

**Month of:** _____ **Day of:** _____ **Year of:** _____

The SLPOA expirations shall expire as indicated above unless revocation occurs by the Principal while in a Healthy State or other methods outlined in **Article IX Subsection B**.

## Article V: Designation of Agent

The Principal should only designate an Agent if that individual is **Reliable**, **Trustworthy**, and **Competent** to manage the Principal's affairs. For legal reasons, all Agents must be competent and at least eighteen (**18**) years or older. None of the following individuals (non-**relative**) may serve as the Principal's Agent. (**A**) Any individual who serves as an Owner, Operator, or employee of a Health Care Facility (Medical, Mental, or Assisted Living) in which the Principal is currently a Patient / Client unless the employee serves solely as a Notary Public. (**B**) Any individual who serves as an Owner, Operator, or employee of a Final Dispositional Facility (Funerary Home, Crematory Authority, and Cemetery Authority) unless the employee serves solely as a Notary Public. (**C**) Any Doctor, Physician, Psychologist, Psychiatrist, Social Worker, Financial Advisor, or Financial Manager in which the Principal is currently a Patient / Client. Automatic Revocation of the Spouse designation as Agent shall occur if the following happens: (**01**) Dissolution or annulment of the marriage. (**02**) Proceedings are currently active for Dissolution of Marriage. (**03**) The Principal currently lives in a separate physical location from their Spouse for more than (**02**) two months with the intention of a divorce. The Principal designates the following individual as the Agent with decision-making powers in adherence to the terms and conditions specified in this SLPOA.

**1ˢᵗ Witness:** _____ **2ⁿᵈ Witness:** _____ **Notary Public:** _____ **Principal:** _____

© 2018 by Paul M. Paquette; Form v3.00
All Rights Reserved; Paquette Publications

Simple Limited
Power of Attorney

You must verify the agent's identity
with a government-issued picture I.D.

Page 02 of 11

**AGENT** →

| | |
|---|---|
| **Full Name:** | |
| **Address:** | |
| **Phone #:** | **Email:** |
| **Residence:** | **County:** **State:** |

In the unlikely event that the Agent refuses, is unable, or is denied (by a Judge or Principal) to act as an Agent. The Principal dictates that this SLPOA has expired and that the SLPOA's effectiveness and legitimacy be invalid, null, and void.

# Article VI: Health Status Definitions

**A: Incapacitation** shall occur if a court of competent jurisdiction has issued a court order stating that the Principal is incapacitated. Alternatively, the Principal currently has a medical and mental health condition diagnosed by (**02**) two licensed independent Physicians who have personally examined the Principal. Under the penalty of perjury, the Physicians stated in writing that the Principal demonstrates one or more of the following conditions. (**01**) The Principal cannot make, participate, or communicate a decision regarding their health care. (**02**) The Principal cannot manage the following: their care, property, or financial affairs. When trying to conceptualize what an incapacitated individual can do, think of an individual unable to control their motor movement and needing help to do regular tasks. Examples include (but are not limited to) the following: Amyotrophic Lateral Sclerosis (ALS), Primary Lateral Sclerosis (PLS), Progressive Bulbar Palsy (PBP), Progressive Muscular Atrophy (PMA), Pseudobulbar Palsy, and Parkinson's disease.

**B: Incompetent** shall occur if a court of competent jurisdiction has issued a court order stating that the Principal is incompetent. Alternatively, the Principal currently has a medical and mental health condition with diagnosis by (**02**) two independent Licensed Health Professionals (any combination will do) that serve in the following capacity (Physician, Clinical Psychologist, or Psychiatrist) who has personally examined the Principal. In writing, the Health Professionals state that the Principal demonstrates one or more of the following under the penalty of perjury. (**01**) The Principal cannot understand and appreciate the extent, nature, and probable consequences of a proposed medical and mental health decision that may or may not have life-sustaining implications. (**02**) The Principal cannot make an informed, intelligent decision in a reasonable amount of time. (**03**) The Principal cannot communicate a coherent decision no matter how simple the communication process is. (**04**) The Principal cannot rationally evaluate the risks and benefits of a proposed medical and mental health decision compared to the risks and benefits of alternatives. Examples include (but are not limited to) the following: Alzheimer's disease, Huntington's disease, Schizophrenia, Psychotic Disorder, and Severe Dementia. **Please Note:** An individual with a mental illness, advanced age, or developmental disability does not automatically imply or constitute a lack of decisional capacity.

**C: Function Non-Socially** shall occur if a court of competent jurisdiction has issued a court order stating that the Principal is functioning non-socially. Alternatively, the Principal currently has a medical and mental health condition diagnosed by (**02**) two licensed independent Physicians who have personally examined the Principal. The Physicians stated in writing, under the penalty of perjury, that the Principal cannot demonstrate one or more of the following: to recognize people, communicate with people, and interact with people in a meaningful way.

**D:** By the term **Healthy**, the Principal means the following: exhibit capacity with complete mental competence, thus fully capable of independent thought and actions, and function socially.

# Article VII: Powers, Rights, Privileges

**Statement from the Principal to the Third Parties:** All Third Parties dealing in good faith with the Agent may fully rely upon the Agent's power and authority to act on the Principal's behalf and in the Principal's name. All Third Parties may accept and rely on agreements and other instruments entered or executed by the Agent under this SLPOA.

**Power and Authority to Acts:** The Agent's powers include the ability to act in the Principal name, place, and stead in any way (in parts or whole) that is proper and prudent. The Agent's powers include acting to the fullest and greatest extent possible in which the Principal is permissible by law to act through an Agent with the Principal's best interest and welfare in mind.

**The Agent's Powers:** The Agent shall have the full power and authority to exercise, perform, manage, and conduct in a fiduciary capacity and shall act with utmost good faith, fair dealing, full disclosure, and fidelity towards the Principal. The Agent shall have any incidental rights required to conduct and perform the specific powers granted herein. The Agent shall exercise the Principal legal rights and powers, including those rights and powers that the Principal may acquire in the future.

**1st Witness:** _____ **2nd Witness:** _____ **Notary Public:** _____ **Principal:** _____

**DIRECTIONS:** The Principal must **place "Y"** for **Yes** in all applicable empty box spaces below and initial "✐" on **the line** for activation of Agent's Power(s). The Principal must **place "N"** for **No** to all applicable empty box spaces below **and initial "✐" the line** for no activation of Agent's Power(s). Agent's Power(s) will not receive activation if the empty box space or the Principal's initial is void or left blank.

Place "Y" for Yes or "N" for No in the box and initial "✐" the line if the Principal desires the following:          **(A)**

"Y" or "N" Here ↑          Initial Here ↑          Preferably Type or Legible Writing in Ink for the Description into the above space ↑

**DESCRIPTION:** By designating "Y" for Yes, the Agent's powers include the ability to do the following:

Specify in Detail          Preferably Type or Legible Writing in Ink

Place "Y" for Yes or "N" for No in the box and initial "✐" the line if the Principal desires the following:          **(B)**

"Y" or "N" Here ↑          Initial Here ↑          Preferably Type or Legible Writing in Ink for the Description into the above space ↑

**DESCRIPTION:** By designating "Y" for Yes, the Agent's powers include the ability to do the following:

Specify in Detail          Preferably Type or Legible Writing in Ink

Place "Y" for Yes or "N" for No in the box and initial "✐" the line if the Principal desires the following:          **(C)**

"Y" or "N" Here ↑          Initial Here ↑          Preferably Type or Legible Writing in Ink for the Description into the above space ↑

**DESCRIPTION:** By designating "Y" for Yes, the Agent's powers include the ability to do the following:

Specify in Detail          Preferably Type or Legible Writing in Ink

Place "Y" for Yes or "N" for No in the box and initial "✐" the line if the Principal desires the following:          **(D)**

"Y" or "N" Here ↑          Initial Here ↑          Preferably Type or Legible Writing in Ink for the Description into the above space ↑

**DESCRIPTION:** By designating "Y" for Yes, the Agent's powers include the ability to do the following:

Specify in Detail          Preferably Type or Legible Writing in Ink

**1ˢᵗ Witness:** _____          **2ⁿᵈ Witness:** _____          **Notary Public:** _____          **Principal:** _____

© 2018 by Paul M. Paquette; Form v3.00
All Rights Reserved; Paquette Publications

Simple Limited
Power of Attorney

You must verify the agent's identity
with a government-issued picture I.D.

Page 04 of 11

**Place "Y" for Yes or "N" for No in the box and initial "✎" the line if the Principal desires the following:**

**(E)**

Preferably Type or Legible Writing in Ink for the Description into the above space ↑

"Y" or "N" Here ↑    Initial Here ↑

**DESCRIPTION:** By designating "Y" for Yes, the Agent's powers include the ability to do the following:

*Specify in Detail*

*Preferably Type or Legible Writing in Ink*

---

**Place "Y" for Yes or "N" for No in the box and initial "✎" the line if the Principal desires the following:**

**(F)** Other Terms: (Conditions, Prohibitions, Restriction, Exceptions, Additions, Limitation, Extensions, and Special Rules)

"Y" or "N" Here ↑    Initial Here ↑

**DESCRIPTION:** By designating "Y" for Yes, the Agent's powers may be subject to the following regarding **Other Terms**: conditions, prohibitions, restrictions, exceptions, additions, limitations, extensions, or any special rules as typed in the box below. If there are any contradictions concerning **Article VII Subsections A through E**, the Principal shall type a brief explanation for the contradiction.

*Specify in Detail*

*Preferably Type or Legible writing in Ink*

# Article VIII: Restrictions on Agent's Powers

Regardless of what authorization or powers bestow in **Article VII Subsection A through E,** the Agent shall not do or perform the following: **(01)** The Agent shall not make a loan to oneself, another name Agent, or a beneficiary of the Agent. **(02)** The Agent shall not take a service fee as an Agent. **(03)** The Agent shall not create, modify, or revoke a trust. **(04)** The Agent shall not use the Principal's property to fund a trust for someone other than the Principal or a trust that does not benefit the Principal greater than seventy (70%) percent. **(05)** The Agent shall not create or change a Beneficiary's interest in the Principal's property. **(06)** The Agent shall not create or change the Principal's interest in the Principal's property solely for the benefit of another. **(07)** The Agent shall not designate or change the designation of beneficiaries to receive any property, benefit, or contract right on the Principal's death. **(08)** The Agent shall not make or revoke a gift of the Principal property in trust or another arrangement. **(09)** The Agent shall not make or revoke a gift on the Principal behalf. **(10)** The Agent shall not exercise any powers that would cause the Principal's assets to become taxable to the Agent or the Agent's estate for any income, estate, or inheritance tax. **(11)** The Agent shall not forgive debts owed to the Principal, disclaim, or waive benefits payable to the Principal. **(12)** The Agent shall not execute, publish, declare, amend, or revoke the following: last will, codicil, or any will substitute on the Principal's behalf. **(13)** The Agent shall not perform duties under a contract that requires the Principal's services. **(14)** The Agent shall not make an affidavit about the Principal's knowledge that is unknown to the Agent personally. **(15)** The Agent shall not vote in any governmental public election on behalf of the Principal unless the Agent has a notarized letter stating who the Principal's candidates and voting preferences are regarding that public election. **(16)** The Agent shall not exercise powers and authority granted to the Principal as Trustee or a court-appointed Fiduciary. **(17)** The Agent shall not exercise the right to make a disclaimer on behalf of the Principal, except for a disclaimer of a detrimental transfer or acceptance made with the court's approval. **(18)** The Agent shall not enjoin (add or transfer) ownership or title to the Principal's funds or assets in the Agent's name alone. **Please Note:** Waiver of these restrictions shall only occur if the Principal grants written permission in **Article VII Subsection F.**

1st **Witness:** _____  2nd **Witness:** _____  **Notary Public:** _____  **Principal:** _____

# Article IX: Revocation

**A:** The Principal may revoke the SLPOA in writing for any reason without prior notice to the Agent or any Third Parties. However, in part(s) or whole, any Revocation shall require a Notary Public attesting to the revocation to ensure the authenticity and legitimacy of the Principal's actions.

**B: Revocation Methods:** Revocation of this SLPOA shall only occur in part(s) or whole by the following methods: **(01)** A new SLPOA that states all prior SLPOAs are revoked in writing. **(02)** The Principal revokes the SLPOA in a formal (type) manner with the Principal's signature and notarization. **(03)** The Principal willfully destroys all original (sign and seal) SLPOA and requests the destruction of all copies in writing. **(04)** The appropriate authorities have declared the death of the Principal. **(05)** A court of competent jurisdiction has issued a court order to terminate the Principal's SLPOA, in parts or whole.

**C:** All other Revocation methods shall be invalid and unenforceable, even if they are legally allowable.

# Article X: Durability Provisions

**Statement of Understanding by the Principal:** The Principal understands that the direction and choices implemented by the Agent as specified in this SLPOA (if still active due to durability provision(s) and not previously revoked) shall continue, even if the Principal objects to the actions or decisions later when the Principal is functioning non-socially, incapacitated, or incompetent.

**DIRECTIONS:** The Principal must **place "Y" for Yes** in all applicable empty box spaces below and initial "✐" on **the line** for activation of Durable Power(s). The Principal must **place "N" for No** to all applicable empty box spaces below **and initial "✐" the line** for no activation of Durable Power(s). Durable Power(s) will not receive activation if the empty box space or the Principal's initial is void or left blank.

"Y" or "N" Here ↑    Initial Here ↑    Place "Y" for Yes or "N" for No in the box and initial "✐" the line if the Principal desires the following:    **(A)** **Durability against Incompetence**

**DESCRIPTION:** By designating "Y" for Yes, this SLPOA shall continue if the Principal becomes incompetent; this SLPOA shall survive the effects of incompetence and shall not be invalid, null, or void. Furthermore, the Agent's power and authority shall remain effective when the Principal is incompetent.

"Y" or "N" Here ↑    Initial Here ↑    Place "Y" for Yes or "N" for No in the box and initial "✐" the line if the Principal desires the following:    **(B)** **Durability against Incapacity**

**DESCRIPTION:** By designating "Y" for Yes, this SLPOA shall continue if the Principal becomes incapacitated; this SLPOA shall survive the effects of incapacity and shall not be invalid, null, or void. Furthermore, the Agent's power and authority shall remain effective when the Principal is incapacitated.

"Y" or "N" Here ↑    Initial Here ↑    Place "Y" for Yes or "N" for No in the box and initial "✐" the line if the Principal desires the following:    **(C)** **Durability against Functioning Non-Socially**

**DESCRIPTION:** By designating "Y" for Yes, this SLPOA shall continue if the Principal functions Non-Socially; this SLPOA shall survive the effects of functioning non-socially and shall not be invalid, null, or void. Furthermore, the Agent's power and authority shall remain effective when the Principal functions non-socially.

**Recommendation:** The Agent should attach the **Affidavit of Principal's Health State** by a licensed Health Professional (dated before the expiration date) if the Principal is functioning non-socially, incapacitated, or incompetent when presenting the SLPOA to any Third Party.

1st Witness: _____  2nd Witness: _____  Notary Public: _____  Principal: _____

Simple Limited
Power of Attorney

You must verify the agent's identity
with a government-issued picture I.D.

Page 06 of 11

# Article XI: Ambiguities Interpretation Instructions

**A:** If a provision requires that a specific section be "Type" to be valid, failure to "Type" the section shall make that part invalid, null, and void.

**B:** If a provision requires that a specific section have the **Principal's Initial** for it to be valid, failure to initial the section shall make that part invalid, null, and void.

**C:** If a fillable section is **blank**, thus not typed or filled in, the legal interpretation shall be that the Principal did not intend for that section to be effective, and when it comes to interpreting that section, it shall be invalid, null, and void.

**D:** If a fillable section requires a **Yes "Y"** or **No "N"** and the section is blank (thus not typed or filled in), the legal interpretation shall be that the Principal did not intend for that section to be effective; therefore, it shall be **No "N."**

**E:** If a fillable section requires a **Yes "Y"** or **No "N;"** however, **"Yes"** or **"No"** exists instead, the legal interpretation shall be that the Principal did intend for that section to keep its legal effect and meaning.

**F:** If a fillable section requires a **Check "✓"** and it is blank, thus not typed or filled in, the legal interpretation shall be that the Principal did not intend for that section to be effective; therefore, not wanted.

**G:** If a fillable section gives multiple options that are mutually exclusive to each other in which a **Check "✓"** is required if more than one option is checked "✓" then the legal interpretation shall be that the Principal did this in error; thus when it comes to interpreting that section, the implementation shall be of the more conservative option.

**H:** If a fillable section requires a **Check "✓"** or "X," however a dash "—" exists instead, the legal interpretation shall be that the Principal did not intend for that section to be effective; thus, it is not wanted.

**I:** If a section or provision is typed with added handwritten instructions, only the "typed" section will receive consideration concerning the Principal's intentions. The rationale is simple: any person, not necessarily the Principal, can handwrite (ink in) after the fact. Due to a lack of verification, the additional handwritten instruction shall be invalid, null, and void.

**J:** Most state laws will void a legal document if someone writes on the surface, especially after notarization or execution. The Principal waives this right since the formalization of the SLPOA requires it to be typed and printed; thus, any handwritten alteration concerning the altered section shall be unsubstantial and nonbearing unless an unaltered original duplicate or legitimate copy is available; only the unreadable section shall be invalid, null, and void.

**K:** If this SLPOA allows handwritten statements by the Principal and there seem to be any suspicious alterations or additions (changes in handwriting style, changes in ink), such handwritten alterations or additions shall have no weight or bearing. Unless an unaltered original duplicate or legitimate copy is available, the altered section shall only be invalid, null, and void if it (the altered section) is unreadable as to its original intentions.

**L:** The Descriptions that follow a **Yes "Y"** or a **No "N"** Box are for clarification and informational purposes to outline the performance of duties and rights.

**M:** If a Third Party receives more than one active Power of Attorney regarding the Principal: **(01)** The Power of Attorney that has the most recent date shall take more precedence unless otherwise stated in **Article VII Subsection F**. **(02)** If the Principal function non-socially, incapacitated, or incompetent, then the Power of Attorney that has an active Durability Provision(s), in effect, shall take precedence. **(03)** If the Power of Attorney has the same date, then a General Power takes precedence over a Financial Power of Attorney. A Financial Power of Attorney takes precedence over a Banking Power of Attorney. A Limited Power of Attorney shall be subservient to a General, Financial, and Banking Power of Attorney if any conflicts arise. **(04)** A Protecting Power of Attorney shall stand alone and only be binding upon Complex and Durable Power of Attorney with active Protector provisions. **(05)** A Complex Power of Attorney takes precedence over a Simple Power of Attorney if any conflicts arise. **(06)** Unless otherwise specified within a Special Power of Attorney, a Special Power of Attorney shall take precedence over a Complex and Simple Power of Attorney if there are any conflicts.

# Article XII: Additional Legal Provisions

**A: Reliance by Third Parties:** To induce any Third Party to act, the Principal agrees that any Third Party receiving a duly executed copy/facsimile of this SLPOA may act upon hereunder. The revocation shall be ineffective until the Third Party receives notice or knowledge of the revocation. The Principal, Principal's heir(s), executor(s), administrator(s), legal or personal representative(s), and assign(s) agree to indemnify and hold harmless to the Third Party from and against all claims due to relying upon this SLPOA.

**B: Notice to Third Party:** A Third Party who fails to honor a properly executed SLPOA may be liable to the Principal, the Agent, the Principal's heirs, assigns, or estate. Liabilities may include (but are not limited to) the following: civil penalty plus damages, costs, and fees associated with the failure to comply with the SLPOA.

**C: Compensation:** Any individual serving in a fiduciary capacity in adherence to this SLPOA shall not receive compensation for the performance of their authority, rights, and responsibilities. However, the Fiduciary may receive reimbursement (if possible) for reasonable and necessary expenses incurred in performing their authority, rights, and responsibilities. If the Principal wishes to compensate the Agent, the Principal shall specify in detail in **Article VII Subsection F.**

**D: Binding on Successors:** This SLPOA and all its provisions shall become effective upon execution. All provisions shall be binding upon the heir(s), executor(s), administrator(s), legal or personal representative(s), and assign(s) and all fiduciaries' successors of the Principal as fully allowable by law.

**E: Original Counterparts:** If multiple originals of this SLPOA have been executed, each such counterpart original shall have equal force and effect. Any photocopy of this SLPOA shall have the same force and effect as the original. **Suggestion:** Shade the Notary Public Seal when making a photocopy of SLPOA.

**F: Surety or Bond:** No individual named as an approved Agent selected for consideration by a Judge shall require the filing or furnishing of a bond, surety, or other security in any jurisdiction. If, despite this SLPOA, a bond is necessary, the Principal requests that it be without sureties and in a nominal amount.

**G: Indemnification of Fiduciary:** No individual serving within a fiduciary capacity named in this SLPOA shall incur any liability by the Principal for acting or refraining from acting under this SLPOA except in instances of the Fiduciary's negligence or wanton, willful, or reckless misconduct.

**H: Indemnification of Third Parties:** Third Parties that act in good faith, based on this SLPOA, shall not be subject to liability (criminal or civil) or professional disciplinary action for such reliance, except for the Third Parties' negligence or wanton, willful, or reckless misconduct.

**I: Recordation:** Recording this SLPOA with the county auditor, recording officer, et cetera is permissible, provided it serves a practical legal purpose or reason.

**J: Relative Conflict:** If the approved Agent selected for consideration by a Judge is a Spouse or is an Adult Child/Ward of the Principal. The Principal waives any conflict of interest that their Spouse or Adult Child/Ward might have due to potential inheritance or beneficiary arrangements.

**K: Definition of Child/Ward:** As used in this SLPOA, "Child" shall include any individual the Principal legally adopts. The term "Ward" shall consist of any individual legally in the Principal's care who is also the acting Guardian.

**L: Fiduciaries:** The term Fiduciaries shall include the following: Agent, Medical Health Care Surrogate, Mental Health Care Surrogate, Guardian, or Conservator. Be aware that the Principal reserves the right to designate or nominate other individuals as Fiduciaries in other legal documents to act on the Principal behalf.

**M: Transfer of Fiduciary Powers:** No Agent shall have the rights or powers to any acts, power, duty, right, or obligation relating to any person, matter, transaction, or property in which the Principal is serving as a Fiduciary (Trustee, custodian, or personal representative) for someone else.

**N: Modification:** Upon execution, changes to this SLPOA shall not occur. If the Principal wants to change this SLPOA, the Principal must make an entirely new one. However, revocation of any part(s) of this SLPOA may occur if it is in writing; once a part(s) receives revocation, it shall be permanent. Alterations (strikes out, cross out, and blackouts) of any provisions or writing within this SLPOA shall have no bearing in a court of law and shall remain active and valid as to their original intent.

**O: Picture I.D.:** The Principal requires verifying the Agent's identity with a government-issued picture ID. The Principal does not require it to be current and up to date; all that the Principal requires is the ability to confirm their facial features in a picture from an official governmental source.

**P: Delegation:** The Agent shall not delegate their power or rights to individuals.

1st Witness: _____ 2nd Witness: _____ Notary Public: _____ Principal: _____

**Q: Durability:** If one or more of the durability provisions in **Article X** is active and applicable, then this SLPOA shall remain viable and legally enforceable unless the Principal, while in a Healthy State, implements a Revocation in adherence to **Article IX Subsection B.**

**R: Conflicting Provisions:** If one or more provisions conflict due to the scope and nature of the powers given, the Fiduciary powers shall be reduced in the provision or a subset thereof that is more conservative and prudent in scope and nature.

**S: Headings (Article & Subsection):** Article and Subsection Headings in Bold Face are for informational purposes only and serve as a guide to what the subject entails. However, the heading may not be all-inclusive or reflect all the information about that article, provision, or description. Thus, it behooves the Principal, Agent, and all Third Parties to read the article, provision, or description carefully and with due diligence.

**T: Governing Law:** This SLPOA shall take effect immediately as a sealed instrument and shall receive interpretation, enforcement, and governance under the State's laws where the Principal has established physical residency at the time of enforcement. The Principal requests for the honoring of this SLPOA in any State, County, or Location in which the Principal's body or property may be, with the intention that it be valid in all jurisdictions/territories of the United States and all Foreign Nations. This SLPOA is to receive the most liberal interpretation available to grant the appointed Fiduciary the greatest amount of decision-making discretion.

**U: Severability / Saving Clause:** An invalid or unenforceable provision within this SLPOA might exist. If that occurs, the remaining provisions of this SLPOA shall continue and be active as if said invalid or unenforceable provision did not exist. All remaining provisions shall be undisturbed to maintain their original legal meaning, force, and effect. If a court finds or deems that an invalidated or unenforceable provision will become valid if limitations exist, then such written provision shall receive a written modification by court order to limit the provision's power while maximizing the economic value and liberties granted.

**V: Lapse of Time:** A lapse of time shall not affect the validity or effectiveness of this SLPOA.

**W: Legal Document Priority:** If a court of competent jurisdiction appoints a Guardian or Conservator to oversee and manage the Principal's property, the Principal intended that this SLPOA take precedence over all other means of ascertaining the Principal's intentions. The Principal intends that this SLPOA shall not endure subjugation or subterfuge by any acting Guardian or Conservator unless the area in question is ambiguous. The Guardian or Conservator shall have wide latitude and discretion in their duties in ambiguous cases.

**X: Court Appointed Guardian or Conservator:** the Principal intends by this SLPOA to avoid a court-supervised guardianship or conservatorship. If the Principal attempts or fails to avoid a court-supervised guardianship or conservatorship. Then, the Principal requests that the Agent designated in this SLPOA serve as Guardian or Conservator of the Principal's property and affairs. The court-appointed Guardian or Conservator shall not have the power to revoke, suspend, or terminate this SLPOA or the Agent's powers except as specifically authorized by law. The Principal may execute the following: **"Declaration of Guardianship & Conservatorship,"** if execution occurs, the Principal prefers that those individuals act in such a fiduciary capacity.

**Y: Specific Forms or In-House POA:** If a Third Party refuses to recognize this SLPOA and requires a specific form or in-house Power of Attorney. The Agent can execute said legal document immediately subject to the limitations and rights established in this SLPOA with a permanent attachment of this SLPOA to said document.

1st Witness: _____   2nd Witness: _____   Notary Public: _____   Principal: _____

# Article XIII: Acknowledgment by the Agent

**A:** The Agent shall exercise due care and act in the Principal's best interest with the powers granted while adhering to any limitations, impositions, or specifications within this SLPOA.

**B:** The Agent's foremost duty is loyalty and protection of the Principal and the Principal's interests. The Agent shall direct any benefits derived from this SLPOA to the Principal. The Agent must avoid conflicts of interest and use ordinary skill and prudence to exercise these powers. If there is anything about this SLPOA or the Agent's duties that the Agent does not understand, the Agent shall seek professional advice.

**C:** A court of competent jurisdiction has the discretion to revoke the Agent's power, especially if acting inappropriately. Thus, it behooves the Agent to exercise the bestowed powers in a fiduciary manner. The burden will be upon the Agent to prove that such acts were prudent and within a Fiduciary standard for any questionable acts. The Agent may be liable for damages and subject to criminal and civil prosecution if a court of competent jurisdiction finds that the Agent has violated their fiduciary duty.

**D:** The Agent has the power to abstain from using their granted powers under this SLPOA; however, the Agent does not have the luxury of being negligent when the **Life, Safety**, and **Welfare** of the Principal are at stake. The Agent may be liable for damages, be subject to prosecution (criminal or civil), and suffer termination of powers if a court rules that the Agent has been negligent regarding their fiduciary duty under this SLPOA to the Principal,

**E:** The Agent agrees to keep all monetary funds or financial assets that belong to the Principal in separate accounts from the Agent's monetary funds or financial assets. There shall be no commingling of monetary funds or financial assets to ensure simple accounting and safeguard the Principal's financial security. Furthermore, the Agent agrees to protect, conserve, and exercise prudence and caution in dealings with the Principal's monetary funds, financial assets, and all other assets of value and worth.

**F:** The Agent agrees to keep a complete and accurate record of all acts, disbursements, and receipts for review/inspection. The Agent agrees to provide an accounting/report to the Principal at the following time intervals (as stated below). If the Principal dies, the Executor/Administrator of the Principal's estate shall receive the accounting/report within a quarter. **Directions: Place a "✓" in the Accounting / Report Period box.**

| Report Period: | | None | | Monthly | | Quarterly | | Annually |
|---|---|---|---|---|---|---|---|---|

**G:** By default, the Agent shall not receive compensation for their authority, rights, and responsibilities; however, the Agent may receive reimbursement for reasonable and necessary expenses incurred in performing their authority, rights, and responsibilities. The Principal may compensate the Agent if the Principal desires.

**H:** The Agent shall disclose all actions that require written authorization by using their identity as the Agent in the following manner: (Agent's Signature) as Agent for (Principal's Name).

**I:** For Simple and Special POA, the Agent may resign by notifying the Principal or the Principal's Guardian or Conservator (provided a Judge appoints one). For Complex and Durable POA, the Agent may resign by notifying the Principal, Protector, Co-Agent, Successor Agent, or the Principal's Guardian or Conservator (provided a Judge appoints one). The resignation must be in writing and sent by certified mail, statutory overnight delivery (return receipt requested), or email.

**J:** If the Agent becomes aware of the death of the Principal who executed the SLPOA, the Agent must notify all Third Parties as soon as practicable that the Principal has died and that this SLPOA is no longer legitimate and effective. If Durability Provision(s) are not active or applicable, the Agent must notify all Third Parties as soon as practicable that the Principal is functioning non-socially, incapacitated, or incompetent; thus, the SLPOA is no longer valid.

**K:** If the Agent resigns or ceases to represent the Principal regarding this SLPOA, the former Agent agrees to return all property and documents to the Principal immediately.

**L:** The Agent agrees to keep all information (financial, relationship, or other personal matters) confidential and shall not disclose to any outsiders unless those individuals are relevant Third Parties that require such information.

**M:** The Agent is responsible for informing the Principal of changes in their physical address or contact information.

**N:** If the Durable Provision(s) is active, the Agent may need to sign an Affidavit that the SLPOA is in Full Force and Effect to induce any Third Party to act.

**O:** The Agent accepts this appointment subservient to SLPOA's terms and conditions. The Agent agrees to act and perform reasonably and prudently in a fiduciary capacity with the Principal's best interests in mind. However, the powers granted to the Agent shall expire upon the Principal death. If Durability Provision(s) are not active or applicable, the powers granted to the Agent shall automatically expire if the Principal is functioning non-socially, incapacitated, or incompetent.

**1st Witness:** _____    **2nd Witness:** _____    **Notary Public:** _____    **Principal:** _____

© 2018 by Paul M. Paquette; Form v3.00
All Rights Reserved; Paquette Publications
Simple Limited
Power of Attorney
You must verify the agent's identity
with a government-issued picture I.D.
Page 10 of 11

# Article XIV: Signature and Execution

In the presence of (**02**) two Witnesses and a Notary, the Principal has executed this SLPOA. The Principal understands the full import and meaning of this SLPOA and is aware that this SLPOA gives the Agent **limited powers (written by the Principal) and ability regarding the Principal's property and affairs**. The Principal reaffirms the following in the Witnesses and Notary presence: (**01**) The Principal is at least eighteen (**18**) years or older. (**02**) The Principal is of sound and disposing mind (emotionally and mentally competent) to make or request this SLPOA. (**03**) The Principal has the capacity with full memory or necessary mental faculties to understand and comprehend these actions. (**04**) The Principal willfully and voluntarily executes this SLPOA. (**05**) The Principal declares under the Penalty of Perjury that this paragraph is true and correct.

| Principal → | Full Legal Name: | | Signature: | Thumb/Finger Print: |
|---|---|---|---|---|
| | Today's Date: | | | Real Estate Transaction |

### Have (02) two Adult Witness* the Principal's signature in addition to having their signature notarized*

In the joint presence of each other, the Witnesses State that the Principal is the following: (**01**) The Principal is at least eighteen (**18**) years or older. (**02**) The Principal is of sound and disposing mind (emotionally and mentally competent). (**03**) The Principal is not suffering from constraint, duress, fraud, or undue influence. (**04**) The Principal acknowledges having willfully and voluntarily dated and signed this SLPOA (or asked/directed for such actions to occur). (**05**) The Witnesses affirm that they have no direct biological or marital relationship with the Principal and are not a Beneficiary of the Principal's estate. (**06**) The Witnesses affirm their impartiality and confirm that the criterion stated in the box at the bottom of the last page does not apply. (**07**) The Witnesses declare this paragraph true and correct under the Penalty of Perjury.

### If the Witness is uncomfortable giving out personal contact information, current employment information and occupation will suffice.

| 1st Witness → | Name: | | Signature: |
|---|---|---|---|
| | Address: | | |
| | Phone #: Occupation: | | Date: |

| 2nd Witness Or Special Witness ** → | Name: | | Signature: |
|---|---|---|---|
| | Address: | | |
| | Phone #: Occupation: | | Date: |

1st Witness: _____    2nd Witness: _____    Notary Public: _____    Principal: _____

Simple Limited
Power of Attorney

You must verify the agent's identity
with a government-issued picture I.D.

Page 11 of 11

**UNDER THE
LAWS OF →**

**COUNTY:** _____

**STATE:** _____

Before the Notary Public (the undersigned authority) comes forth, the Principal, with a sound/disposed mind, is eighteen (**18**) years or older. The Principal acknowledges having willfully and voluntarily dated and signed this SLPOA (or asked/directed for such actions to occur) stated above in the Notary Public presence. If Witnesses sign and attest that the Principal has signed this SLPOA, the Notary Public shall attest that the Witnesses have signed this SLPOA in the Notary Public's presence. Furthermore, the Notary Public states that the Principal has provided a Government Issue identification card with a facial picture to prove identity. The Notary Public declares under the Penalty of Perjury that this paragraph is true and correct.

**If the Principal or Witnesses sign this SLPOA but not in the presence of the Notary Public, then the Notary Public will not notarize or sign this SLPOA.**

**\* Notary
Public
→**

| | | |
|---|---|---|
| **Full Name:** | | **Signature & Seal:** |
| **Location:** | | |
| **Address:** | | |
| **Phone #:** | | **I.D. Number:** |
| **Date:** | | **Commission Expires:** |

**\* None shall serve as a Witness, Notary Public, or other qualified individual with the authority to administer oaths regarding this SLPOA made under this section.**

(**01**) Any individual related to the Principal by blood, marriage, or adoption. (**02**) Any individual currently a Beneficiary of the Principal's estate (laws of intestate succession or any existing will/codicil). (**03**) Any individual who benefits from a financial policy (insurance or annuity) in which the Principal's life is insured. (**04**) Any individual claiming (present/inchoate) any part of the Principal's estate. (**05**) Any individual who serves as an Owner, Operator, or employee of a Health Care Facility (Medical, Mental, or Assisted Living) in which the Principal is currently a Patient / Client unless the employee serves solely as a Notary Public. (**06**) Any Doctor, Physician, Psychologist, Psychiatrist, Social Worker, Financial Advisor, or Financial Manager in which the Principal is currently a Patient / Client. (**07**) Any individual who serves as an Owner, Operator, or employee of a Final Dispositional Facility (Funerary Home, Crematory Authority, and Cemetery Authority) unless the employee serves solely as a Notary Public. (**08**) Any individual who is an Agent (active/inactive) serving in a fiduciary capacity under this SLPOA. (**09**) Upon the Principal's death, any individual or entity with a claim (the creditor) against the Principal's estate. (**10**) Any individual under eighteen (**18**) years or is incapacitated or incompetent. The Witnesses should be twenty-one (**21**) years of age or older.

**Special Witness\*\*** If the Principal is a resident of a sanitarium, rest home, nursing home, boarding home, et cetera, it is highly beneficial that a patient advocate or ombudsman be one of the Witnesses while executing this SLPOA.
**Legal Questions:** Consult the State laws or contact a licensed Attorney.

**1st Witness:** _____ **2nd Witness:** _____ **Notary Public:** _____ **Principal:** _____

# This page is intentionally left blank

# This page is intentionally left blank

# This page is intentionally left blank

# This page is intentionally left blank

# This page is intentionally left blank

# This page is intentionally left blank

# This page is intentionally left blank

PUBLICATIONS

PAQUETTE

"The true man is revealed in difficult times." ~ Epictetus

**Broom Peddler – 1737** [1, 2 & 3]

**Well Cleaner – 1746** [1 & 2]

**Lettuce Seller – 1742** [1 & 2]

**Hurdy-Gurdy Player – 1737** [1 & 2]

**Fish Vendor – 1738** [1, 2 & 3]

**Young Milkmaid – 1737** [1, 2 & 3]

# Image Source

Photo

"Love Family
Heart Parent"

Marcela

June 26, 2015

Photo ID: 826936

CC License
from Pixabay

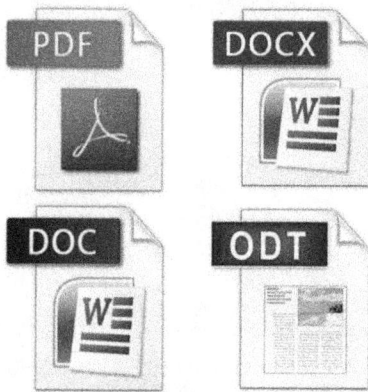

Graphic Art

(DOC, PDF, DOCX)

Jordan M. Groll

2008

(ODT)

Paul M. Paquette

2018

Use with
Permission
Jgroll.com

Graphic Art

Star of Life
Blue Version

Rod of Asclepius,
with Snake around it

Philippe Verdy

2006

Wikimedia
Commons

Graphic Art

Paquette
Publications
Logo by
Paul M. Paquette

2018

# Image Source

Photo

**"Drumsticks Sticks Drums Music"**

**Christian Plass**

**May 11, 2016**

**Photo ID:** 1377492

- **Simple POA** is for short-term (less than five years) use with an Agent whose honor is beyond reproach and doubt. The Simple POA has only one additional (**01**) option/safety feature: **Durability Provision**, hence the name "**Simple**." If Durability Provisions are active, this POA will also qualify as a "**Durable POA.**"

  - **Key Details:** Names only one Agent, Effective Immediately, Define Expiration Date, and Built-In Safety Features
  - **Option:** Durability Provisions

- **Complex POA** is for long-term (greater than five years) use, preferably with multiple Agents to reflect the changing realities of life. These multiple options/safety features, if implemented, will create an administrative burden by establishing checks and balances on the Agent's power, hence the name "Complex." If Durability Provisions are active, this POA will also qualify as a "**Durable POA.**" If Springing Power(s) are active, this POA will also qualify as a "**Springing POA.**"

  - **Key Details:** Names Multiple Agent with successor's Agent, Variable Effective Date, Variable Expiration Date, Built-In Safety Features, and Sprinkling Powers
  - **Options:** Durability Provisions, Springing Powers, Agent Co-Power Sharing, Protector Provision, Delegate Provision, and Security Footer Settings.

- **Durable POA** is, in essence, a Complex POA, but with one key difference: the Durability Provisions are already active; thus, the durability provision is a "Key Detail" instead of an "Option." By default, the Durable POA will never have a simpler version due to the nature of the subject matter. This POA qualifies as a "**Durable POA.**" If Springing Power(s) are active, this POA will also qualify as a "**Springing POA.**"

- **Special POA** is, in essence, a Simple POA, best used sparsely with a limited scope and purpose. By default, the Special POA will never have a more complex version due to the nature of the subject matter. If Durability Provisions are active, this POA will also qualify as a "**Durable POA.**" This POA is also referenced as a "**Limited POA.**"

# Power of Attorney

**1st Edition**
Abridged Version

Visual Forms within are intended
for Illustration Purposes

# Simple Banking
# Power of Attorney

Power of Attorney (POA only)
for Your Estate Planning Needs

(Requires Internet)
Downloadable
Files

Paul M. Paquette

**Preview the entire book in advance
at www.Legal-POA.com**

---

**1st Edition**
Abridged Version

Visual Forms within are intended
for Illustration Purposes

# Complex Banking
# Power of Attorney

Power of Attorney (POA only)
for Your Estate Planning Needs

(Requires Internet)
Downloadable
Files

Paul M. Paquette

**Preview the entire book in advance
at www.Legal-POA.com**

---

**1st Edition**
Abridged Version

Visual Forms within are intended
for Illustration Purposes

# Simple Financial
# Power of Attorney

Power of Attorney (POA only)
for Your Estate Planning Needs

(Requires Internet)
Downloadable
Files

Paul M. Paquette

**Preview the entire book in advance
at www.Legal-POA.com**

---

**1st Edition**
Abridged Version

Visual Forms within are intended
for Illustration Purposes

# Complex Financial
# Power of Attorney

Power of Attorney (POA only)
for Your Estate Planning Needs

(Requires Internet)
Downloadable
Files

Paul M. Paquette

**Preview the entire book in advance
at www.Legal-POA.com**

# Power of Attorney

## Simple General Power of Attorney

Power of Attorney (POA only)
for Your Estate Planning Needs

(Requires Internet)
Downloadable Files

Paul M. Paquette

Preview the entire book in advance
at www.Legal-POA.com

## Complex General Power of Attorney

Power of Attorney (POA only)
for Your Estate Planning Needs

(Requires Internet)
Downloadable Files

Paul M. Paquette

Preview the entire book in advance
at www.Legal-POA.com

## Simple Limited Power of Attorney

Power of Attorney (POA only)
for Your Estate Planning Needs

(Requires Internet)
Downloadable Files

Paul M. Paquette

Preview the entire book in advance
at www.Legal-POA.com

## Complex Limited Power of Attorney

Power of Attorney (POA only)
for Your Estate Planning Needs

(Requires Internet)
Downloadable Files

Paul M. Paquette

Preview the entire book in advance
at www.Legal-POA.com

# Power of Attorney

## Simple Real Estate Power of Attorney

Power of Attorney (POA only)
for Your Estate Planning Needs

(Requires Internet)
Downloadable Files

Paul M. Paquette

Preview the entire book in advance
at www.Legal-POA.com

## Complex Real Estate Power of Attorney

Power of Attorney (POA only)
for Your Estate Planning Needs

(Requires Internet)
Downloadable Files

Paul M. Paquette

Preview the entire book in advance
at www.Legal-POA.com

## Simple Power of Attorney for Minor Child

Power of Attorney (POA only)
for Your Estate Planning Needs

(Requires Internet)
Downloadable Files

Paul M. Paquette

Preview the entire book in advance
at www.Legal-POA.com

## Complex Power of Attorney for Minor Child

Power of Attorney (POA only)
for Your Estate Planning Needs

(Requires Internet)
Downloadable Files

Paul M. Paquette

Preview the entire book in advance
at www.Legal-POA.com

# Power of Attorney

## Durable Protecting Power of Attorney

Power of Attorney (POA only)
for Your Estate Planning Needs

(Requires Internet) Downloadable Files

Paul M. Paquette

Preview the entire book in advance at www.Legal-POA.com

## Durable Power of Attorney for Final Disposition (Funeral & Burial)

Power of Attorney (POA only)
for Your Estate Planning Needs

(Requires Internet) Downloadable Files

Paul M. Paquette

Preview the entire book in advance at www.Legal-POA.com

## Durable Power of Attorney for Health Care

Power of Attorney (POA only)
for Your Estate Planning Needs

(Requires Internet) Downloadable Files

Paul M. Paquette

Preview the entire book in advance at www.Legal-POA.com

## Durable Power of Attorney for Health Care of Minor Child

Power of Attorney (POA only)
for Your Estate Planning Needs

(Requires Internet) Downloadable Files

Paul M. Paquette

Preview the entire book in advance at www.Legal-POA.com

# Power of Attorney

# Declarations

## Declaration of Guardianship & Conservatorship

Legal Forms for your Estate Planning Needs with Supporting Documents

(Requires Internet) Downloadable Files

Paul M. Paquette

Preview the entire book in advance at PaquettePublications.com

## Declaration of Guardianship & Conservatorship for Minor Child

Legal Forms for your Estate Planning Needs with Supporting Documents

(Requires Internet) Downloadable Files

Paul M. Paquette

Preview the entire book in advance at PaquettePublications.com

## Declaration of Guardianship & Conservatorship for the Disabled

Legal Forms for your Estate Planning Needs with Supporting Documents

(Requires Internet) Downloadable Files

Paul M. Paquette

Preview the entire book in advance at PaquettePublications.com

## Declaration of Final Disposition (Funeral & Burial)

Legal Forms for your Estate Planning Needs with Supporting Documents

(Requires Internet) Downloadable Files

Paul M. Paquette

Preview the entire book in advance at PaquettePublications.com

# Declarations

# Advance Directives

## Advance Medical Health Directive

**Advance Medical Health Directive**

Legal Forms for your Estate Planning Needs with Supporting Documents

(Requires Internet) Downloadable Files

Paul M. Paquette

Preview the entire book in advance at PaquettePublications.com

## Advance Mental Health Directive

**Advance Mental Health Directive**

Legal Forms for your Estate Planning Needs with Supporting Documents

(Requires Internet) Downloadable Files

Paul M. Paquette

Preview the entire book in advance at PaquettePublications.com

## Do Not Resuscitate Advance Directive (DNR)

**Do Not Resuscitate Advance Directive (DNR)**

Legal Forms for your Estate Planning Needs with Supporting Documents

(Requires Internet) Downloadable Files

Paul M. Paquette

Preview the entire book in advance at PaquettePublications.com

# Relationship Agreements

## Prenuptial Agreement

Legal Forms for your Estate Planning Needs
with Supporting Documents

(Requires Internet)
Downloadable Files

Paul M. Paquette

Preview the entire book in advance
at PaquettePublications.com

## Postnuptial Agreement

Legal Forms for your Estate Planning Needs
with Supporting Documents

(Requires Internet)
Downloadable Files

Paul M. Paquette

Preview the entire book in advance
at PaquettePublications.com

## Prenuptial Agreement
### For Same-Sex Marriage

Legal Forms for your Estate Planning Needs
with Supporting Documents

(Requires Internet)
Downloadable Files

Paul M. Paquette

Preview the entire book in advance
at PaquettePublications.com

## Postnuptial Agreement
### For Same-Sex Marriage

Legal Forms for your Estate Planning Needs
with Supporting Documents

(Requires Internet)
Downloadable Files

Paul M. Paquette

Preview the entire book in advance
at PaquettePublications.com

# Relationship Agreements

## 1st Edition — Visual Forms within are intended for Illustration Purposes

# Prenuptial Agreement
## for Civil Union / Partnership

Legal Forms for your Estate Planning Needs
with Supporting Documents

(Requires Internet)
Downloadable Files

Paul M. Paquette

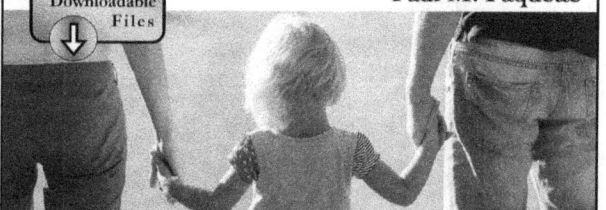

Preview the entire book in advance
at PaquettePublications.com

## 1st Edition — Visual Forms within are intended for Illustration Purposes

# Postnuptial Agreement
## for Civil Union / Partnership

Legal Forms for your Estate Planning Needs
with Supporting Documents

(Requires Internet)
Downloadable Files

Paul M. Paquette

Preview the entire book in advance
at PaquettePublications.com

## 1st Edition — Visual Forms within are intended for Illustration Purposes

# Custodial Agreement
## for Minor Child

Legal Forms for your Estate Planning Needs
with Supporting Documents

(Requires Internet)
Downloadable Files

Paul M. Paquette

Preview the entire book in advance
at PaquettePublications.com

## 1st Edition — Visual Forms within are intended for Illustration Purposes

# Visitation Agreement
## for Minor Child

Legal Forms for your Estate Planning Needs
with Supporting Documents

(Requires Internet)
Downloadable Files

Paul M. Paquette

Preview the entire book in advance
at PaquettePublications.com

# Relationship Agreements

## Guardianship Agreement for Minor Child

Legal Forms for your Estate Planning Needs with Supporting Documents

(Requires Internet) Downloadable Files

Paul M. Paquette

Preview the entire book in advance at PaquettePublications.com

## Guardianship Agreement for Disabled Adult

Legal Forms for your Estate Planning Needs with Supporting Documents

(Requires Internet) Downloadable Files

Paul M. Paquette

Preview the entire book in advance at PaquettePublications.com

## Cohabitation Agreement

Legal Forms for your Estate Planning Needs with Supporting Documents

(Requires Internet) Downloadable Files

Paul M. Paquette

Preview the entire book in advance at PaquettePublications.com

## Domestic Partnership Agreement

Legal Forms for your Estate Planning Needs with Supporting Documents

(Requires Internet) Downloadable Files

Paul M. Paquette

Preview the entire book in advance at PaquettePublications.com

# Relationship Agreements

## Separation Agreement

Legal Forms for your Estate Planning Needs
with Supporting Documents

Paul M. Paquette

Preview the entire book in advance
at PaquettePublications.com

## Reconciliation Agreement

Legal Forms for your Estate Planning Needs
with Supporting Documents

Paul M. Paquette

Preview the entire book in advance
at PaquettePublications.com

## Word Processor Program

The Purchaser or User can open, edit, print, and save the Digital Files using a word processing program. Popular Word Processing Programs include Microsoft Word, WordPerfect, Open Office, and Libre Office. All word processing forms come in the following (**DOC**, **DOCX**, **ODT**). Paquette Publications does not offer the Word Processing Program or Technical Support for the Word Processor Program.

## Portable Document Format (PDF) Editor

The Purchaser or User can open, edit, print, and save the Digital Files using a PDF Editor program. Popular PDF Editor include Adobe Acrobat Pro, Nitro Pro 11, PDF-Xchange Editor, Master PDF Editor, and CutePDF Writer. Paquette Publications does not offer the PDF Editor or Technical Support for the PDF Editor. Adobe Acrobat Reader is free to download at **www.adobe.com**. **Please Note:** due to encryption standards of **256-bit AES**, this PDF is only backward compatible (read/write) with **Adobe Acrobat X or later**.

## Printer Setting

Depending on the printer's capabilities and settings, the Digital File (**DOC**, **DOCX**, **ODT**) may need editing to prevent cut-off text from occurring near the margins. The easiest way to solve this problem is to verify that the printer and margin settings are correct. If you still have issues, edit/fill out the Digital File, convert it, and save it as a **PDF** file. PDF files are easier, more versatile, and present fewer errors when printing. Paquette Publications does not offer Printing capabilities or Technical Support for Printers.

## Modification Recommendation

If the Purchaser or User plans to make changes to the Digital File in question, it is highly advantageous that the Purchaser or User utilize the (**DOC**, **DOCX**, or **ODT**) file format. If the Purchaser or User is content with the choice selection, provisions, and options currently available with minor changes (if applicable), then it is highly recommended that the Purchaser or User utilize the **PDF** file format.

# Downloadable Digital Files

## Legal Disclaimer:

The Forms presented in this Book are available as a direct download from **www.paquettepublications.com**. In adherence with **Copyright Laws**, **Licensing Agreements**, and **Legal Disclaimers & Waivers**, these forms and their files are for personal and immediate family use only.

## Legal Disclaimer required by the Distributor:

This Book does not have digital files (**PDF**, **DOCX**, **DOC**, and **ODT**) attached and does not contain fillable files or forms. As a courtesy, the Author has provided an Active URL Link to download the digital file (**PDF**, **DOCX**, **DOC**, **ODT**); however, the Purchaser or User will need to have an internet service connection, computer access, appropriate software, printing capabilities, and the ability and willingness to access the Author's website.

## File Format Options:

The Digital Files are in the following formats: Microsoft Office Word (**DOC**, **DOCX**), Adobe Acrobat (**PDF**), and Open Office (**ODT**). The **PDF**, **DOCX**, **DOC**, and **ODT** are fillable and editable with the appropriate computer software.

## Consent Checkbox:

To download these Digital Files (**PDF**, **DOCX**, **DOC**, and **ODT**), the Purchaser or User must first consent to the following Terms and Conditions (**Legal Disclaimer & Waivers**, **Licenses & Trademark**, and **All Rights Reserved**) which are present on the website.

# Terms & Conditions

> ☐ **By checking this box, the Purchaser or User has read and agree to the following:** Legal Disclaimers & Waivers, License & Trademark, **and** All Rights Reserved **before downloading these file(s) (PDF, DOCX, DOC, ODT).**
>
> submit

## Download Links:

Using an internet browser (**Chrome**, **Edge**, **Explorer**, **Firefox**, and **Safari**), the Purchaser or User can download the Forms (**PDF**, **DOCX**, **DOC**, and **ODT**) presented within this Book from the following active URL Links:

**Power of Attorney:**
- https://paquettepublications.weebly.com/tc---spoa21---poa49.html

**Supporting Documents:**
- https://paquettepublications.weebly.com/agrave-la-carte.html

**Worksheets:**
- https://paquettepublications.weebly.com/agrave-la-carte.html

**Forms (Miscellaneous):**
- https://paquettepublications.weebly.com/agrave-la-carte.html

**Forms (Recommended):**
- https://paquettepublications.weebly.com/agrave-la-carte.html

**Appendices & Glossary:**
- https://paquettepublications.weebly.com/free---appendix.html

**Extras:**
- https://paquettepublications.weebly.com/free---extra.html

# CD / DVD

This CD / DVD is designed (built and formatted) to work with Microsoft's Windows Operating System but should also work on Apple's Macintosh Operating System. **Please Note:** Paquette Publications does not provide technical support for computers or operating systems.

Print on Demand (POD) book
will have no CD / DVD available.

Please refer to the **"Downloadable Digital Files"** page to access the file(s) (PDF, DOCX, DOC, and ODT).

**Please Return Disc with Book**

www.ingramcontent.com/pod-product-compliance
Lightning Source LLC
Chambersburg PA
CBHW051229200326
41519CB00025B/7308

* 9 7 8 1 9 4 8 3 8 9 6 9 3 *